Star Trek and the Philosophy of Entertainment

PETER LANG
PROMPT

George A. Gonzalez

Star Trek and the Philosophy of Entertainment

Beauty, Justice, and Popular Culture

PETER LANG
Lausanne • Berlin • Bruxelles • Chennai • New York • Oxford

Library of Congress Cataloging-in-Publication Data

Names: Gonzalez, George A., author.
Title: Star Trek and the philosophy of entertainment: beauty, justice, and popular culture / George A. Gonzalez.
Description: New York: Peter Lang, 2023. | Includes bibliographical
references and index. | Identifiers: LCCN 2023004316 (print) | LCCN 2023004317 (ebook)
| ISBN 9781636671550 (hardback) | ISBN 9781636671567 (ebook) |
ISBN 9781636671574 (epub)
Subjects: LCSH: Star Trek television programs. | Star Trek films–History
and criticism. | Justice, Administration of, on television. | Justice,
Administration of, in motion pictures. | Popular culture–Philosophy. |
LCGFT: Television criticism and reviews.
Classification: LCC PN1992.8.S74 G655 2023 (print) | LCC PN1992.8.S74
(ebook) | DDC 791.45/75–dc23/eng/20230316
LC record available at https://lccn.loc.gov/2023004316
LC ebook record available at https://lccn.loc.gov/2023004317
DOI 10.3726/b20623

Bibliographic information published by the **Deutsche Nationalbibliothek.**
The German National Library lists this publication in the German
National Bibliography; detailed bibliographic data is available
on the Internet at http://dnb.d-nb.de.

Cover design by Peter Lang Group AG

ISBN 9781636671550 (hardback)
ISBN 9781636671567 (ebook)
ISBN 9781636671574 (epub)
DOI 10.3726/b20623

© 2023 Peter Lang Group AG, Lausanne
Published by Peter Lang Publishing Inc., New York, USA
info@peterlang.com - www.peterlang.com

All rights reserved.
All parts of this publication are protected by copyright.
Any utilization outside the strict limits of the copyright law, without the permission of the
publisher, is forbidden and liable to prosecution.
This applies in particular to reproductions, translations, microfilming, and storage and
processing in electronic retrieval systems.

This publication has been peer reviewed.

For Ileana and Alana

CONTENTS

Chapter 1   A Philosophy of Entertainment   1

Chapter 2   The Cases of Nazi Cinema and the American war in Vietnam   19

Chapter 3   The Progressive Politics of 1950s Sci-Fi Movies and Star Trek of the 1960s   37

Chapter 4   *Star Trek* (Original Series) at the Center of the Justice (Values) Revolution of the 1960s   49

Chapter 5   Star Trek and the Progressive Dialectic: The Depiction of the Marxist Ontology of Justice   61

Chapter 6   *The Boys* and *Justice League Unlimited*: The Super Hero as Metaphorical of Global (In)Justice   67

Conclusion   Popular Culture as Prime Political Terrain in the Struggle for Democracy/Justice   85

Bibliography 89
Index 105

· 1 ·

A PHILOSOPHY OF ENTERTAINMENT

I have written numerous volumes on the philosophy and political theory that informs popular culture (television shows, movies)—with a particular emphasis on the Star Trek franchise.[1] My most recent monograph on the intersection between philosophy, political theory, and popular culture invokes the Hegel/Marx *political philosophy* paradigm.[2] The focus of this volume is the *philosophy of art*—especially popular culture. The Hegel/Marx paradigm yields a *metaphysics of beauty* (entertainment), and a conception of *justice* that allows for an understanding of popular culture.

---

1 George A. Gonzalez, *The Politics of Star Trek: Justice, War and the Future* (New York: Palgrave Macmillan, 2015), *The Absolute and Star Trek* (New York: Palgrave Macmillan, 2017), *Star Trek and the Politics of Globalism* (New York: Palgrave Macmillan, 2018), *Justice and Popular Culture: Star Trek as Philosophical Text* (Lanham, MD: Lexington Books, 2019), *Popular Culture and the Political Values of Neoliberalism* (Lanham, MD: Lexington Books, 2019), *Popular Culture as Art and Knowledge* (Lanham, MD: Lexington Books, 2019), *Popular Culture, Conspiracy Theory, and the Star Trek Text* (Lanham, MD: Lexington Books, 2020), and *Star Trek and Popular Culture: Television at the Frontier of Social and Political Change in the 1960s* (New York: Peter Lang, 2021).
2 George A. Gonzalez, *Star Trek and Star Wars: The Enlightenment versus the Anti-Enlightenment* (New York: Peter Lang, 2022).

The *absolute*, philosophized upon most saliently by Georg Hegel (1770–1831),[3] is the driving force behind history.[4] Reality is composed of the Absolute—encompassing the laws of physics and the normative values that shape human values and behavior. From the Absolute, we can deduce a theory of beauty. It is key to note that the Absolute and reality operate as an ontological process (not as a static thing), as well as dialectically. Art is the depiction of the dialectical ontology of reality. Thus, art is the engagement of the *spirits* of the Absolute. The spirits comprise our sensory reality—hard, soft, red, green, gravity, trees, rocks, etc., as well as normative values that animate human behavior (greed, fairness, kindness, etc.). The spirits operate dialectically and are manifest in endless, numerous combinations. Humans seek out these endless combinations—that is the basis of art (including popular culture). Immanuel Kant wrote of the Dialectical Image—the idea that classification (categorization) of objects, values are in dialogue with art. Classification shapes art, and art also impacts upon classifications (our understanding of categories).[5]

As I argue in *The Absolute and Star Trek*, rationality in Star Trek, as for Hegel, is found not in reducing the absolute to an object (a system of categorization, a formula, or prophetic text), but in understanding the ontology of the absolute—i.e., reality as process, not as a thing.[6] The *Star Trek: Next Generation* (1987–1994) episode "Justice" (1987) expressly rejects prophetic morality (divine rules) when one of the Enterprise crew violates a "law" handed down by the deity of planet. The society and the deity demand that the divine rules be upheld to the letter, which would result in the execution of the Enterprise crew member. (The crew member unknowingly and accidentally violated a forbidden area.) What can be interpreted as a critique of

---

3 Donald Phillip Verene, *Hegel's Absolute: An Introduction to Reading the Phenomenology of Spirit* (Albany: State University New York Press, 2007); Stephen Houlgate, *Hegel's 'Phenomenology of Spirit': A Reader's Guide* (New York: Bloomsbury Academic, 2013); James Kreines, *Reason in the World: Hegel's Metaphysics and Its Philosophical Appeal* (New York: Oxford University Press, 2015).

4 Robert L. Perkins, ed., *History and System: Hegel's Philosophy of History* (Albany: State University of New York, 1984); Will Dudley, ed., *Hegel and History* (Albany: State University of New York Press, 2009).

5 Immanuel Kant, *Critique of the Power of Judgment*, rev. ed. (New York: Cambridge University Press, 2001[1790]). Also see Mike Wayne, "The Dialectical Image: Kant, Marx and Adorno," in *Marx at the Movies: Revisiting History, Theory and Practice*, E. Mazierska and Lars Kristensen, eds. (New York: Palgrave Macmillan, 2014).

6 Gonzalez, *The Absolute and Star Trek*.

Kant's Categorical Imperative, Captain Picard argues to the deity "that there can be no justice so long as laws are absolute."[7] First Officer Riker adds "when has justice ever been as simple as a rulebook?"

The Star Trek text conveys Hegelian metaphysics in the *Voyager* (1995–2001) episode "Sacred Ground" (1996). In this episode a direct reference to the existence of "spirits" is made—as noted above a term Hegel himself would use to denote something beyond material existence (e.g., the physical laws [spirits] of gravity, conservation, thermal dynamics; also, the *spirits* of love, morality, happiness, etc.).[8] During the episode, the following is said to Captain Janeway: "Mathematics. I can see why you enjoyed it. Solve a problem, get an answer. The answer's either right or wrong. It's very *absolute*." A veiled reference to Hegel's philosophy? Indicative of Hegelian reasoning the following point is made: "Real is such a relative term." Janeway's *material realist* thinking (only matter and energy exist) is described in the following: "That would be nice and quantifiable for you, wouldn't it. If the spirits were something you could see and touch and scan with your little devices." Overtly critiquing Kantian rationalism,[9] the following is said to Janeway: "There you go again, always looking for a rational explanation. Well, there isn't one."

The action of "Sacred Ground" centers on the fact that Voyager crew member, Kes, becomes incapacitated when she comes into contact with an "energy field." Voyager's doctor is unable to bring Kes out of her coma and she's on the verge of death. Unable to find a scientific explanation for the field or Kes's condition, Captain Janeway is forced to appeal to the "monks" that oversee the energy field. They consider it a manifestation of their deities—the *Ancestral Spirits*. In order to save Kes, Janeway is told "that the only thing that matters is finding your connection to the spirits." In the end, it is only when Janeway accepts that something beyond material reality exists (i.e., the *Ancestral Spirits*) that Kes is revived.

Abstract Expressionism (a 20th century phenomenon) decisively moves *philosophy of art* towards Hegelian metaphysics. What the viewer is in fact seeing in Abstract Expressionism is color theory in action—absent any

---

7 T. C. Williams, *The Concept of the Categorical Imperative: A Study of the Place of the Categorical Imperative in Kant's Ethical Theory* (New York: Clarendon Press, 1968).

8 Robert B. Brandom, *A Spirit of Trust: A Reading of Hegel's Phenomenology* (Cambridge, MA: Belknap, 2019).

9 In the *Critique of Pure Reason*, Kant argues that reason and empiricism can account for all phenomena. Immanuel Kant, *Critique of Pure Reason*, trans. Max Muller (New York: Penguin, 2008 [1781]).

categorization of items, ideas, politics, etc. The artwork of such painters as Jackson Pollock, Willem de Kooning in essence is depicting, capturing the beauty that humans *see* in particular colors juxtaposed (contrasted), along with *pleasing* patterns (or what can be deemed anti-patterns). Why do we humans find any particular interaction of colors, (anti-) patterns *beautiful*? A similar observation can be made of Impressionist paintings—perhaps Van Gogh most saliently.Classicist Henry Paolucci explains that "art" (along with religion and philosophy) "are in the end, for Hegel, 'moments' of *absolute spirit*."[10] Similarly, philosopher William Desmond, in A *Study of Hegel's Aesthetics: Art and the Absolute*, notes that "Art has an *absolute* dimension; indeed, it belongs together with religion and philosophy itself as one of the three highest modes of human meaning."[11] While the Hegelian approach to art is cast as a means to look upon art (along with religion and philosophy) as a means to understand the absolute—in other words, as a source of knowledge (epistemology),[12] my emphasis here is to argue that the absolute allows us to understand art and what exactly is art. So in philosophically pondering Van Gogh's Starry Night, or a Pollock or a Wassily Kandinsky art piece, and asking why do we humans find such interactions of colors, lines *beautiful?*—the answer is the *absolute*. Hegelian philosophy would point to the *spirit of beauty*. Therefore, artistic talent is the ability to invoke, channel the *spirit of beauty*—color theory, etc.[13]

This is the negation of artistic tastes as culturally, sociologically, or even psychologically, based. Of course, artistic trends, tastes can be (are) influenced, shaped by cultural, historical trends—that are to at least some degree place based. But we mustn't interpret any specific place-based artistic trends as operating in isolation—as all can appreciate beauty (regardless of cultural upbringing, specific influences). This is perhaps most especially true of art that is aesthetics *qua* aesthetics—art absent political, philosophical, historical motifs. In other words, Starry Night, Pollock, Kandinsky are ostensibly

---

10 Henry Paolucci, "Introduction" in *Hegel: On the Arts*, Henry Paolucci, ed., 2nd ed. (Smyrna, DE: Griffon House, 2001), xix, emphasis added.
11 William Desmond, *Art and the Absolute: A Study of Hegel's Aesthetics* (Albany: State University of New York Press, 1986), xii, emphasis added.
12 Lydia L. Moland, *Hegel's Aesthetics: The Art of Idealism* (New York: Oxford University Press, 2019).
13 Roger Sructon, *Beauty: A Very Short Introduction* (New York: Oxford University Press, 2011); Guy Sircello, *New Theory of Beauty* (Princeton: Princeton University Press, 2016); Aaron Fine, *Color Theory: A Critical Introduction* (New York: Bloomsbury, 2021).

the most universal of art/artists. Additionally, in our current globalized world artistic trends tend to be global—at a minimum influenced by art and ideas from various parts of the world.

Hegel himself held that art during his time had become subservient to aristocratic, religious hierarchies. Certainly, it is the case that in the late 18th and early 19th centuries the European art scene did not reflect the rational, secularism that was reflected in the American (1775–1783) and French (1789) Revolutions. Instead, Renaissance art was dominated by religious, aristocratic motifs.[14] Nonetheless, Renaissance art can be only fully understood (I submit) if it is viewed as in dialogue (or in opposition) to the secular, humanist values that began with the Enlightenment—coming fully to a head in the 17th, 18th, and 19th centuries—that accompanied the Renaissance (14th to 19th centuries).[15] Thus, even if it is skewed in conservative (status quo) directions, Renaissance art was dialectical to the Enlightenment. What we see in Renaissance paintings is a polemic against humanism and secularism—an argument in favor of Christianity and the monarchy. The suffering, torturing of Christ is graphically depicted (*Christ Carrying the Cross*, the *Crucifixion*), as is the suffering of Mary in holding her dead son (the *Lamentation*). These are arguments as to why these figures—demigods—warrant our fealty, subservience. There are also paintings of monarchs, aristocrats in direct contact with God, apostles, saints—and Jesus and Mary are also frequently crowned (indicating that monarchy is the form of governance ordained by the celestial heavens).

The *spirit of justice* informs our perception of beauty. Through multiple volumes I've drawn on Hegel's insights on art to analyze, understand the spirit of justice—knowledge thereof. Yet, I believe there is insight to be gained to understanding the process in reverse—how justice influences what is deemed to be beautiful. The historic (and perhaps contemporary) aesthetic power of Christian-related Renaissance art is that Jesus, etc. are the embodiment

---

14 Geraldine A. Johnson, *Renaissance Art: A Very Short Introduction* (New York: Oxford University Press, 2005); Gordon Campbell, ed., *The Oxford Illustrated History of the Renaissance* (New York: Oxford University Press, 2019); Katherine Giuffre, *Outrage: The Arts and the Creation of Modernity* (Stanford: Stanford University Press, 2023).

15 Jonathan I. Israel, *Radical Enlightenment: Philosophy and the Making of Modernity, 1650–1750* (New York: Oxford University Press, 2001), *Enlightenment Contested: Philosophy, Modernity, and the Emancipation of Man, 1670–1752* (New York: Oxford University Press, 2006), and *The Expanding Blaze: How the American Revolution Ignited the World, 1775–1848* (Princeton: Princeton University Press, 2017).

of justice, fairness. Renaissance art is important and distinct in that what is depicted is justice. Put differently, Jesus et al. are not solely depicted/imposed—in other words, these are gods, deities to worship. Instead, Renaissance art can more fruitfully be read as making arguments as to the justice, fairness of Christianity. For instance, it is reasonable to hold that the mural at the front of the Sistine Chapel is beautiful in significant part because of the message it depicts—namely, that Jesus will (fairly) dispense justice on Judgment Day (with Jesus motioning the good, pious to heaven and others to hell). Four examples of progressive Renaissance painting motifs: (1) *The Adoration of the Magi*; (2) *The Adoration of the Shepherds*; (3) *Jesus Talks with the Samaritan Woman at the Well*; and (4) *Jesus and the Adulteress*. All four reflect Biblical stories. The Adoration of the Magi represents the idea that Christianity is a universal religion (as opposed to a tribal one). Kings from different corners of the world (conveyed through the skin tone of the three monarchs) visit Jesus upon his birth—honoring him with precious gifts. Baby Jesus happily welcomes them. Seemingly every significant museum collection of Renaissance art has at least one rendition of the Magi—normally many. The Adoration of the Shepherds (shepherds fawning over baby Jesus) is also fairly common and can be read in tandem with the Magi motif—as Jesus is also the savior of the common man (not only the aristocracy, the monarchy). The Samaritan motif is less common. Nonetheless, it is significant because it too conveys the universal justice of Christianity. A Samaritan expresses surprise that Jesus would talk to her because the Samaritans and the Israelis are at odds. Jesus, however, only sees people (not political allegiance/identity). The Adulteress depicts an episode in the life of Jesus. An adulteress is brought to Jesus by a vengeful crowd in order to dispense punishment, but Jesus famously withholds judgment—instead declaring "Judge Not Lest Ye Be Judged" (don't judge/condemn others for their personal imbroglios).

Justice and Popular Culture

With Renaissance art we are still in the realm of aesthetic *qua* aesthetic as much of the artistic appeal of such art is still found in color theory, etc. Among all visual art forms it is in popular culture (movies, television) that justice or injustice is unambiguously at the center of the "beauty" (or entertainment value) of art. (Horror movies are ironically about justice insofar as the "horror" of these movies is precisely the total absence of justice—in the face of wanton, gory violence and mayhem.[16]) Certainly, audiences are drawn to the physical beauty, charisma of actors. Additionally, cinematography (and musical score) contributes to the artistry of movies, television episodes. Invariably, however, it is plot that determines the artistic success, popularity (entertainment value) of any particular instantiation of popular culture.

Perhaps the most common plot line in all of popular culture is the crime drama—usually involving the police. The center of this expansive genre is (criminal) justice.[17] Justice in this instance is twofold: first, audiences want to see people animated by the crimes that are depicted. In other words, they want to see (violent) crime taken seriously and perpetrators aggressively pursued—protagonists seeking justice for victims (and their families, friends). More than justice, audiences want to know the truth underlying any and all crimes portrayed—even if the perpetrators evade punishment.

Truth is seemingly a virtual universal in all of popular culture. Audiences not only want to know the truth, but they want characters to pursue the truth. The movie *The Matrix* (1999) is noteworthy on this score. At the center of the movie is class conflict (metaphorically)—as machines have conquered humanity and are using humans for their body heat as an energy source. In order to manage humans, the machines have induced a collective hallucination—whereby people falsely believe they are living lives in modern society. The movie makes direct reference to post-modernism—suggesting that humanity is in actuality immersed in a world of illusion. (The post-modern position is that popular culture takes on greater psychological, political proportions than reality itself). Striking against post-modernism, however, is the claim in the movie that there is a reality (an *objective truth*) to know—the world where humans are reduced solely to objects.[18] The philosophically significant aspect of the plot is that audiences want the protagonists to succeed and uncover the truth for the whole of humanity—hopefully, freeing humans from their enslavement. The reason this is of particular significance in *The Matrix* is because the Earth has been ecologically devastated and people would certainly live a fuller, richer life in the collective hallucination created by the machines than they would in actual reality. Nevertheless, the protagonists and the

---

16 Thomas Fahy, ed., *The Philosophy of Horror* (Lexington: University of Kentucky Press, 2012).
17 Gonzalez, *Popular Culture as Art and Knowledge*, chap. 6.
18 Tony Burns, "Marxism vs. Postmodernism: The Case of *The Matrix*", in *Red Alert: Marxist Approaches to Science Fiction Cinema*, Ewa Mazierska and Alfredo Suppia, eds. (Detroit: Wayne State University Press, 2016).

audience find the situation where humanity is maintained in a delusional state intolerable. The plot is motivated by the (seemingly universal) sentiment that people must know the truth and seek to overcome an unjust circumstances (in other words, realize justice)—irrespective of the consequences.

The plot of the *Matrix* closely mirrors that of the *Star Trek* (1966–1969) unaired pilot—"The Cage" (later aired as part of the episode "The Menagerie" 1966). "The Cage" is more philosophically lucid in terms of ascribing to humanity an insuperable drive for truth, freedom, justice. An advanced alien race (Talosians) capable of inducing detailed, realistic hallucinations wants to enslave the Enterprise crew. The Talosians come to conclude, however, that humans are unsuitable for their project: "The customs and history of your race show a unique hatred of captivity. Even when it's pleasant and benevolent, you prefer death. This makes you too violent and dangerous a species for our needs."

Outside of horror movies, even the most trite/frothy/light of movies, television episodes have characters that treat others with kindness—at a minimum politeness. Additionally, audiences expect those that are rude, dishonest, insincere, etc. to lose out or somehow get their comeuppance. This was the leitmotif of *Seinfeld* (1989–1998)—whereby the four lead characters' slight misdeeds would somehow, improbably catch up with them.[19] Arguably, one of the great disappointments of modern American television is that the character Frank Underwood doesn't "pay" for his terrible crimes committed on his unlikely path to the U.S. presidency—series *House of Cards* (2013–2018). Underwood personally murdered people; had others murdered; as well as destroyed lives; but because the actor Kevin Spacey who played Underwood was accused of sexual misconduct the character was killed off prior to the final season of the series.[20] The result being that Underwood never suffered the consequences of his vicious, dastardly skullduggery.

The profound challenge for the creators of popular culture is to portray the structural injustices of (capitalist) society, and offering solutions (denouements) that are credible and result in just/fair/uplifting outcomes. Rag to riches narratives—viewed as cliché—were/are a means to depict poverty, deprivation and nonetheless have a conclusion whereby the characters are able to financially thrive—if not become very wealthy. Another artistic approach is to

---

19 Maya Salam, "Years Later, 'Seinfeld' Resonates," *New York Times*, May 15, 2023, C1.
20 Christopher Kuo, "Kevin Spacey, Facing Trial in London, Plans a Return to Acting," *New York Times*, June 16, 2023, C4.

depict a mass movement that politically (overcomes) confronts the injustice, inequality of society. This scenario is presented in the *Star Trek: Deep Space Nine* (1993–1999) episode "Past Tense" (1995). In this episode, lead characters unwittingly go back in time to 2024 San Francisco. What they encounter are "Sanctuary Districts"—walled off urban zones where untold numbers of the poor, economically displaced are forcibly interned. The audience is told that there are such districts in every major U.S. city. The episode is centered on what would be the Bell Uprising—whereby mass demonstrations, rioting precipitates the profound, progressive reform of society (more on the *Deep Space Nine* episode "Past Tense" in chapter five).

The de-industrization of what would become the Rust Belt[21] is at the center of the 1977 movie *Slap Shot*. The steel mill that sustains a town in Pennsylvania is shutting down—throwing the town's residents into economic crisis. In this context (hockey) rules and sexual norms (repression) break down.[22] The key dramatic action of the movie is when the lead character confronts the owner of the minor league hockey team he plays for. She informs him that despite the recent competitive and financial success of the team she's shutting it down—for tax purposes. In the face of her callous indifference he verbally lashes out at her—not an actual solution. In the end, the hockey player gains a coaching job elsewhere and he's empowered to hire some of his former teammates. Other characters are off to parts unknown.

On the question of the portrayal of economic despair the show *Roseanne* (1988–1997, 2018) is noteworthy. Lead characters, Dan and Roseanne, find themselves jobless and with no source of income—unable to pay bills (their electricity is cut off) ("The Dark Ages" 1992). The series *Roseanne* is significant insofar as its creators sought to convey the financial uncertainties and dead-end jobs of the lower middle class. Two breadwinners of a family in the late 1980s and 1990s living in the Rust Belt (small town Illinois) with a sudden loss of income ending up homeless was not a distinctive phenomenon. Nevertheless, to have the Conner family literally on the street was seemingly too depressing a turn for the creators of the show. They use a *deus ex machina* solution that seemed out of place for the series, and the narrative shifts away

---

21 Tracy Neumann, *Remaking the Rust Belt: The Postindustrial Transformation of North America* (Philadelphia: University of Pennsylvania Press, 2016); Jason Hackworth, *Manufacturing Decline: How Racism and the Conservative Movement Crush the American Rust Belt* (New York: Columbia University Press, 2019).

22 For a full treatment of the movie *Slap Shot*, see Grant Wiedenfeld, *Hollywood Sports Movies and the American Dream* (New York: Oxford University Press, 2022), chap. 3.

from that of a family of five (Dan, Roseanne, and their three children) on the verge of being homeless. Roseanne's mother loans her money to open a diner, and the family's financial crisis disappears ("Looking for Loans in All the Wrong Places" 1992).

The *Equalizer* (2021–) episode "True Believer" (2021) is about the putative political perils of the vast income gap that dominates the American economy.[23] An unemployed, impoverished worker turns to a right-wing extremist group and terrorism—planning to bomb a building that serves as "a magnet for foreign students" in New York City. The worker is motived by the unfairness he perceives resulting from contemporary capitalism and the existence of what is popularly known as the Billionaire Class[24]: "The banks, the hedge funds forcing people like me from our jobs so they can squeeze out a few more bucks.... I can't put food on my family's table.... They're making billions."

Idealism and Popular Culture

Hegel viewed social, political progress as resulting from the evolution of ideas (idealism) – nationhood overcoming tribalism; citizenship rights replacing arbitrary royal power; rational/fair judicial processes as opposed to prejudice. In popular culture a common motif is the personal (political/social) growth of the individual—i.e., the socially, politically backward ideas that dominate characters' thinking shifts over time to more progressive, humane, accepting ones. One prominent example (in the widely read *The Adventures of Huckberry Finn*) is that of Huckberry Finn—who overcomes the vile, myopic ethnic ("race") hatred of the antebellum South to embrace the humanity of his AfricanAmerican friend (Jim). An example of a television character evolving/changing is that of Archie Bunker—initially from the television show *All in the Family* (1971–1979), later the series *Archie Bunker's Place* (1979–1983). When the character of Archie Bunker is first introduced he is persistently (insultingly) racist, sexist, homophobic—as well as jingoistically pro-American and pro-Catholic. Much of the *All in the Family* comedy

---

23 Thomas Piketty, *Capital in the Twenty-First Century*, trans. Arthur Goldhammer (Cambridge, MA: Belknap Press, 2014).

24 Benjamin I. Page, Jason Seawright, and Matthew J. Lacombe, *Billionaires and Stealth Politics* (Chicago: University of Chicago Press, 2018); Peter S. Goodman, *Davos Man: How the Billionaires Devoured the World* (New York: Custom House, 2022); Anand Giridharadas, "Warren Buffett and the Myth of the 'Good Billionaire'," *New York Times*, June 14, 2021, A23.

(especially early in the show) is putatively derived from Archie's ignorance, backwardness—including the butchering of the English language. Over the course of 12 seasons, encounters with people from different walks of life do leave an imprint on Bunker. The character softens with regard to hostility toward anyone who is different from him—in the process expressing revulsion of the KKK (*All in the Family*—"Archie and the KKK" 1977) and showing sincere respect toward Judaism (both *All in the Family*—"Stretch Cunningham, Goodbye" 1977 and "The Appendectomy" 1979). The Bunker character never abandons his conservative views. Nevertheless, in *Bunker's Place* his relationship with his young adopted Jewish daughter takes more center stage than his caustic views, comments.

Another 1970s television show character that notably *softens* over time is the *Three's Company* (1977–1984) character of Mr. Furley. Furley is Jack Tripper's apartment building manager. In order to be able to live in the building with his two female roommates Jack has to pretend to be gay. Furley when first introduced is openly homophobic and hostile to Jack. Over time, while not renouncing homophobia, Furley does come to value Jack's friendship.

A counter example to the political progression of characters is the case of George Jefferson—from the television show *The Jeffersons* (1975–1985). George, an African American and the lead character, maintains a salient racialist attitude during the entirety of the series—consistently using the racial epithet of "Honky" (to comedic effect) to deride "whites". The episode "George and the President" is noteworthy on two scores—first, in the episode (which aired in 1976) a discussion of the American Revolution occurs. In this discussion George and his wife, Louise, argue that African Americans had essentially nothing to do with the *Declaration of Independence* (1776)—except as servants, etc. in Independence Hall (where the document was signed). The implication is that African Americans have a profoundly, distinctly different history from "whites". The other outstanding issue in this episode is George's explicit racism. He is using his last name to falsely advertise that he is a direct descendant of Thomas Jefferson in an effort to increase business to his chain of dry cleaners. When George, however, is invited to go on television to tout his fake lineage he ends up rejecting the entire project because he's repulsed at the idea that the world would think that he's related to "white" people. What may be more significant is George's family taps into his racism as a way to get him to drop the falsehood that he's related to Thomas Jefferson—as they are uncomfortable with the deception (even for only advertising purposes). The message being that "black" racism is acceptable.

The broadest depiction of the social/political evolution (or ongoing *elevation*) of humanity is outlined in the Star Trek franchise. Interestingly, in the Star Trek franchise the evolving rationality, maturity of humanity is referred to most explicitly in *Star Trek: The Animated Series* (1973–1974). The episode "The Magicks of Megas-Tu" (1973) invokes the Salem witch trials. Old world "devils, warlocks, evil sorcerers" were the misunderstood, maligned, massacred aliens (Megans) that the Enterprise was now encountering. The Megans now fearful of humans, place Kirk *et al.* on trial: "These are the defendants, as representatives of the vilest species in all the universe, treacherous humanity." In humanity's defense Kirk explains: "in the centuries since the Salem witch trials, we have learned. We try to understand and respect all life forms.... The records of the Enterprise are open for your inspection. All the history of Earth and the Federation is at your disposal." In an effort to tap into the prejudices of humans, the Enterprise crew is told that the one Megan that has befriended, protected them is no less than "the Rollicker, the Tempter, Lucifer" himself. Kirk, reflecting modern, secular, humane reasoning, retorts: "We're not interested in legend. He's a living being, and intelligent life form. That's all we have to know about him. We will not join in harming him." The Megans decide to imprison Lucifer for eternity for aiding the Enterprise. Kirk risks death to protect, help Lucifer: "I have to, or you'll become as bad as the Earthmen you fear. You're acting out of terror instead of out of thought or respect." This convinces the aliens that humans have indeed evolved: "The Megans had to have proof that mankind had grown and learned wisdom since they last saw Earth. Your compassion was that proof, Captain." "The Eye of the Beholder" (1974) is an episode where Kirk *et al.* end up as specimens in the zoo of a highly advanced species. Ultimately, Kirk's captors conclude that the Enterprise crew doesn't belong in a zoo because humans "are considered simplistic, but in the process of evolving into a higher order." Spock (who can engage in telepathic communication with the aliens) goes on to explain "it seems they were where we are some tens of thousands of centuries ago." Similarly, in the episode "Bem" (1974) an advanced alien creature recognizes that humans have evolved in terms of rationality, intellect: (to Kirk et al.):

> Punishment? What is punishment? Revenge? Intelligent beings need no revenge. Punishment is necessary only where learning cannot occur without it. You are behind that. My children here [a primitive peoples the entity oversees] are not. That is why you must leave, so as not to corrupt their development with concepts that they are not yet ready for.

The dichotomy between ancient people and modern humanity is again referenced in "How Sharper Than A Serpent's Tooth" (1974). A powerful creature (Kukulkan) that visited Earth thousands of years ago is again visiting Earth and demanding the deference (worship) that he received from primitive humans: "You are my children. I hoped I could teach you, help you." Kirk: "You did, long ago, when it was needed most. Our people were children then. Kukulkan, we've grown up now. We don't need you anymore." Realizing the validity of Kirk's argument, Kukulkan, deflated: "I will let you go your own way. I have already done what I can."

Class Conflict and Beauty

Karl Marx (1818–1883) focused his analysis of capitalism on the relationship between economic classes (capitalists and workers)—with the *means of production* (i.e., the infrastructures through which the production of commodities takes place) at the center of this relationship. Therefore, the *means of production* and *economic classes* operate dialectically—natural resources, technology, economic interests (including political conceptions of justice, fairness) interact—thereby collectively shaping the operation of society. For Marx, social, political progress results from this dialectic—i.e., the *progressive dialectic*. Juxtaposed to Hegelian idealist reasoning, Marx's approach is labeled *materialist*.[25]

Diego Rivera's (1886–1957) artistic success is the result of his ability to translate the Marxist *progressive dialectic* into murals—his most well-known works. These murals depict social, technological, political progress—relatively primitive societies evolving into technologically advanced ones. This evolution is impelled as a direct result of the interaction of the forces of reaction with the forces of progress. Rivera celebrates the revolutions of the 18th and 19th centuries in the mural of "Pan America Unity" (1940)—conveying the history of the western hemisphere. In this history Rivera inserts the figures of Washington, Jefferson, Lincoln, John Brown, and Bolivar. Rivera also depicts the forces of reaction—Hitler, Stalinism (making reference to the killing of Leon Trotsky by a Stalin agent). Perhaps Rivera's most famous (or infamous) mural is "Man at the Crossroads" (1933)—where he translates

---

25 Gareth Stedman Jones, *Karl Marx: Greatness and Illusion* (Cambridge: Cambridge University Press, 2016); Tom Rockmore, *Marx's Dream: From Capitalism to Communism* (Chicago: University of Chicago Press, 2018).

Rosa Luxemburg's (1915) pronouncement ("the future is either socialism or barbarism") into visual art. In this mural two different visions of society are represented: on the right side is the triumph of socialism (V.I. Lenin and Leon Trotsky—leaders of the Russian Revolution) and societal harmony, whereas on the left are capitalists foregrounding rampant militarism and police repression. Within the capitalist barbarism side of the mural are also images of progress—advanced agriculture (various types of crops); science (the theory of evolution); advanced technology (an x-ray machine); and young students from various backgrounds learning (public education). Therefore, within capitalism are both forces, factors of repression, immense violence as well as of social, scientific, technological progress. Thus, Rivera (who was a prominent member of the Mexican Communist Party), like Marx, is not seeking to demonize capitalism (per se), but (on its face) depicting the (the economic, political) development of society in a manner consonant with Marxism—an (ideal) endpoint of social, political evolution being communist society (modern classless society, totally free of ethnic, gender biases).[26] In Rivera's mural "History of Mexico" (1935) is the figure of Karl Marx (pointing to the future).

At the analytical core of Marxism is modern (capitalist) society as class struggle: hegemonic capitalist elites pursue their interests at the expense of the public good and the public (workers) resisting their victimization. The economic exploitation and political repression at the heart of class relations (according to Marx) is pointedly depicted in the *Star Trek* (original series) episode "The Cloud Minders" (1969). The Enterprise visits the planet of Ardana. Through effective imagery the political/economic/social realities of the planet are portrayed—with the privileged/governing caste living a life of aesthetic splendor in a "cloud city" ("Stratos") floating in the heavens; on the (barren) planet surface are where the laboring classes (referred to as "Troglytes") live—working the mines (extracting "zenite"). Perhaps in the most classical Marxist disquisition in all of popular culture, Mr. Spock (first officer of the Enterprise) (through voice over) describes the stark class exploitation and acute class conflict of Ardana:

> This troubled planet is a place of the most violent contrasts. *Those who receive the rewards are totally separated from those who shoulder the burdens....* Here on Stratos, everything is incomparably beautiful and pleasant.... [T]he harsh life in the mines is instilling the people with a bitter hatred. The young girl who led the attack against us when we beamed down was filled with the violence of desperation.

26 Peter Singer, *Marx: A Very Short Introduction* (New York: Oxford University Press, 2001).

Torture, as well as racism, are deployed in an effort to break a political movement in opposition to the governing regime. A prisoner is pressed to provide the names of the putative leaders of the mining caste's rebellion: "You still refuse to disclose the names of the other Disrupters." "There are no Disrupters!" "Very well, if you prefer the rays." She screams in agony, discomforting onlookers. Spock, in his famous calm, equanimous voice, observes that "Violence in reality is quite different from theory."

> But what else can [Troglytes] understand, Mister Spock?
> All the little things you and I understand and expect from life, such as equality, kindness, justice.
> Troglytes are not like Stratos dwellers, Mister Spock. They're a conglomerate of inferior species.

Ardana's leader complains that (because of Captain Kirk's efforts at reform) he "knows nothing except how to destroy our power."

The *Star Trek: Next Generation* episode "Transfigurations" (1990) also depicts political, military elites seeking to suppress the elevation of humanity. "John Doe", as he regains his memories and bearings, is finally able to transform into seemingly the *whole*—the absolute. (John: "my species is on the verge of a wondrous evolutionary change. A transmutation beyond our physical being. I am the first of my kind to approach this metamorphosis." "My people are about to embark upon a new realm, a new plane of existence." The character is cast as possessing a quality of peace and kindness. (Dr. Crusher to John: "I don't believe you're capable of harming any[one]."

In contrast to John Doe, who seemingly achieves the ideal balance between emotion and reason (or zen) and ostensibly comes to completely know (perhaps become) the absolute, Commander Sunad of Zalkon—who demands John be killed—is dominated by "fear" of social change. ("The Zalkonians are afraid of John.") They are fearful that John's transformation is subversive. Sunad charges that John "is a disruptive influence. He spreads lies. He encourages dissent. He disturbs the natural order of our society." (John: Zalkon's "leaders... claimed we were dangerous so they destroyed anyone who exhibited the signs of the transfiguration.")

Sunad's fear prevents him from embracing the fact that John has achieved a higher plane of existence, and when John offers him the knowledge of this existence ("Let me show you") Sunad rejects it ("Don't touch me!"). Sunad "feels personally threatened by John." Thus, Sunad's instrumental reason[27] (i.e., his desire for political authority; high social status; and social/political stability as an end unto itself) prevents him from literally seeing/knowing the absolute.

Glaringly, Donald J. Trump, as U.S. President (2017–2021), declaimed *"that America will never be a socialist country"*[28]—thereby manifesting a hate of social justice. Additionally, as President, Trump openly promoted (twittered) "white power"[29]—i.e., racism. Trump actively animated far right elements throughout his presidency—culminating with the storming of the U.S. Capitol Building on Jan. 6th, 2021.[30] More broadly, Republican elected leaders have recently threatened with violence those they perceive as advocates for "socialism"—i.e., social justice.[31] The third season (2021) of the Amazon Prime series *Hanna* (2019 to 2021) depicts a secret government program targeting 20 twenty-something year olds for assassination because they are perceived as potential ("subversive"[32]) leaders of future change—the presumed theory is to preemptively kill would-be Lenins, Trotskys, etc.

---

27 Darrow Schecter, *The Critique of Instrumental Reason from Weber to Habermas* (New York: Bloomsbury Academic, 2012); Max Horkheimer, *Critique of Instrumental Reason*, trans. Matthew O'Connell (New York: Verso, 2013 [1974]).
28 As quoted in Anita Kumar "Decoding Trump's speech before the United Nations," *Politico*, Sept. 24, 2019. Web.
29 Michael D. Shear, "Trump Amplifies 'White Power' on Twitter," *New York Times*, June 29, 2020, A15.
30 Denver Riggleman, and Hunter Walker, *The Breach: The Untold Story of the Investigation into January 6th* (New York: Henry Holt, 2022); Julian E. Zelizer, ed., *The Presidency of Donald J. Trump: A First Historical Assessment* (Princeton: Princeton University Press, 2022).
31 Editorial Board, "Ms. Greene Is Beyond the Pale," *New York Times*, Feb. 1, 2021, A20; Jonathan Weisman, and Catie Edmondson, "Republican Censured By a Divided House For a Violent Video," *New York Times*, Nov. 18, 2021, A14; Jonathan Weisman, "Boebert's Call to Ilhan Over 'Suicide Bomber' Remark Shows Chasm Between Parties," *New York Times*, Nov. 30, 2021, A20; Alan Feuer, "Gun-Toting Candidate's Ad Suggests Hunt for 'RINOs'," *New York Times*, June 21, 2022, A17; Jennifer Valentino-DeVries, and Steve Eder, "Trump Backers Use 'Devil Terms' to Rally Voters," *New York Times*, Oct. 23, 2022, A1.
32 "Look Me In the Eye" 2021—*Hanna* (Amazon Prime)

Conclusion and Book Overview

In the 20th century two sustained projects of militarism were unable to utilize popular culture to "sell" their respective public on the *justice* of these efforts. I'm referring to the German Nazi's regime of warmongering, hate, and genocide, as well as the American war in Vietnam (wherein the U.S. military measured success by the number of enemy dead[33]—the same metric the Nazis used for the Holocaust). The fact that neither the German film industry, nor American media companies, put forward (broadly speaking) movies, television shows seeking to rally support for their countries' politics, military campaigns (Germany in the 1930s and 1940s and the U.S. in the 1960s and 1970s) communicates two salient points: first, it serves to substantiate my claim that at the heart of popular culture is the *spirit of justice* and, second, neither of these military, political projects were informed by justice (Chapter 2).

Another politically *dark* chapter in modern history is the anti-communist witch-hunts of the 1950s in the U.S. During this decade a number of outer space science fiction movies were released. One argument is that these movies reflected the anti-communism of the times. Juxtaposing these movies with *Star Trek* of the 1960s, I hold these movies in fact philosophically reflect the Enlightenment and should be read as a negative commentary on the anti-communist turn of the period (Chapter 3).

It is because justice (and its pursuit) is beautiful (entertaining) that the Star Trek franchise is seemingly the most popular in history. A fictional collective shift in public reasoning toward social justice is outlined in *Star Trek* (original series) when in the episode "City on the Edge of Forever" (1967) Captain Kirk explains to Edith Keeler in the context of the 1930s that *"Let me help. A hundred years or so from now a famous novelist will write a classic using that theme. He'll recommend those three words even over I love you."* The diminishment of *I love you* reflects the rejection of the kind of self-centeredness emblematic of capitalism—in other words, the individual's desire for love (to love and be loved), wealth, prestige, personal power. This kind of self-regarding is at the core of instrumental reason.[34] The embrace of *let me help* over *I love you* is to center human consciousness on societal well-being—spurning individual aggrandizement (ego-gratification) in favor of the

---

33 Harry G. Summers, "Body Count Proved to Be a False Prophet," *Los Angeles Times*, Feb. 9, 1991, A5; Gregory A. Daddis, *Westmoreland's War: Reassessing American Strategy in Vietnam* (New York: Oxford University Press, 2014).

34 Schecter, *Critique of Instrumental Reason*; Horkheimer, *Critique of Instrumental Reason*.

welfare of others, society. *Star Trek* (original series) saliently represented justice for women and African Americans. Hence, it was arguably at the center of the values revolution of the 1960s and 1970s (Chapter 4). More broadly, Star Trek is the artistic embodiment of the Hegel/Marxist progressive dialectic—history resulting in a modern, classless society (totally free of ethnic, gender biases) (Chapter 5).

The superhero genre has been about justice since its inception in the 1930s—fighting crime and the nefarious plots of super-villains. Two iterations of this genre engage the matter of justice in a distinctive manner. *Justice League Unlimited* depicts superheroes as a metaphor for global justice. The creators of *The Boys* utilize the trope of the superhero as a means to critique the authoritarianism of corporate global power (Chapter 6)

· 2 ·

THE CASES OF NAZI CINEMA AND THE AMERICAN WAR IN VIETNAM

The Frankfurt School holds that popular culture is a means to repress and manipulate the public.[1] Jonas Staal, in *Propaganda Art in the 21st Century*, seeks to establish the field of what he labels *Propaganda Art Studies*. Staal asserts that hegemonic institutions/groups by definition produce art that is deemed to be propaganda: "propaganda art as the performance of power as art";[2] holding that there are "three elements of... propaganda art...: the control over infrastructure [including television and movie production, distribution], the control over narrative, and the control over imagination."[3] It is reasonable to read into Staal's argument that hegemonic institutions/groups are near all-powerful when it comes to shaping public opinion (broadly) through popular art—exercising "control over imagination".

---

1 Jere Paul Surber, *Culture and Critique* (New York: Routledge, 1998), chap. 5; David Gartman, *Culture, Class, and Critical Theory: Between Bourdieu and the Frankfurt School* (New York: Routledge, 2012); Paul Jones, *Critical Theory and Demagogic Populism* (Manchester: Manchester University Press, 2021); Grant Wiedenfeld, *Hollywood Sports Movies and the American Dream* (New York: Oxford University Press, 2022), chap. 1.
2 Jonas Staal, *Propaganda Art in the 21st Century* (Cambridge, MA: MIT Press, 2019), 1.
3 Staal, *Propaganda Art in the 21st Century*, 9.

The Frankfurt School adherents' and Staal's ostensive claim of the instrumentally of art can seemingly be made with regard to Renaissance art (paintings, sculptures), as such art collectively failed in the 14th to early 19th centuries to adequately, fully reflect the humanism and rationality that was becoming dominant (the Enlightenment)—as manifest by the American (1775—1783) and French Revolutions (1789). Instead, art (particularly in the artistically dominant European scene) was entrenched within religious, mythological motifs.[4] This is not to deny that art during this period became more sophisticated and beautiful (one wants to say impassioned) in presenting arguments supportive of religion (Christianity) and the aristocracy. Nevertheless, art in this context can be viewed as a rearguard action by hegemonic elites to counter the enlightenment process that was taking place. The art world in this period was dominated by wealthy patrons and wealthy connoisseurs—not to the mention the official and brutal censorship at the time.[5]

With movies and television, art (culture), however, took a decidedly popular turn. For popular culture to reach/affect the public, it has to be authentic. Put differently, to get people to watch movies, television shows they have to appeal to them (i.e., they have to be popular). Popular culture can be deemed the democratization of culture—art for the masses. Thus, even though the movie and television industries are dominated by major, behemoth corporations and the Billionaires that own and control them,[6] popular culture cannot solely reflect their outlook and political/social preferences. Instead, popular culture (to a significant degree) must convey broader reasoning on political/social phenomena, and even be a venue of critique of hegemonic groups, institutions.

A recent salient example of such critique is the animated movie *Superman: Red Son* (2020). In this iteration of the Superman franchise the "Man of Steel" is a Soviet citizen and an adherent of the October Revolution. Superman comes to learn of Stalin's perfidy and murders him—taking over leadership of the country. Superman ends Stalinist repression, but the regime

---

4 Evelyn Welch, *Art in Renaissance Italy: 1350–1500* (New York: Oxford University Press, 2001); Susie Nash, *Northern Renaissance Art* (New York: Oxford University Press, 2009).

5 James Simpson, *Permanent Revolution: The Reformation and the Illiberal Roots of Liberalism* (Cambridge, MA: Belknap, 2019); Eric Berkowitz, *Dangerous Ideas: A Brief History of Censorship in the West, from the Ancients to Fake News* (Boston: Beacon Press, 2021).

6 Eli M. Noam, and The International Media Concentration Collaboration, *Who Owns the World's Media?: Media Concentration and Ownership around the World* (New York: Oxford University Press, 2016).

uses mind control to maintain obedience and in the end the "Soviet empire" is dissolved. The distinctive critique in the movie is that of American foreign policy. Under the leadership of capitalist Lex Luther, the U.S. carries out unprovoked aggression against the Soviet Union (a.k.a. the USSR)—a false flag downing of a satellite on Manhattan and unleashing "superheroes" against it (thereby attacking the USSR). Perhaps especially significant, Luther develops a "Superior Man" to counter Superman. When Superior Man is introduced to the public he declares "America First"—suggesting that U.S. anti-Soviet policy (anti-communism) at the center of the Cold War was informed by virulent nationalism.[7] The German Nazis would similarly like to emphasize "Germany above all else" (Deutschland über alles).[8] In actual history the U.S. did attack the Soviet Union in the context of the country's civil war,[9] violated its air space with spy planes,[10] and maintained a hostile foreign policy toward the USSR in the form of an aggressive military posture.[11] In *Red Son* the Berlin Wall is deployed by the West—a metaphor for the anti-Soviet policy of *containment*?[12]

The inability to use popular culture in an instrumental manner is evident with Nazi cinema and the American war in Vietnam. What I will show is that popular culture could not be used in either case in an effective manner to manipulate or stupify the public because at the core of movies, television shows is the *spirit of justice*. Popular culture in the absence of this spirit is perceived as propaganda—i.e., spurious. In the case of the Nazis they consciously wanted to use the cinema to explain that their vile politics of hate and white supremacy was the embodiment of the spirit of justice. In the end they couldn't

---

7 George A. Gonzalez, *Star Trek and Popular Culture: Television at the Frontier of Social and Political Change in the 1960s* (New York: Peter Lang, 2021), chap. 2.

8 Daniel A. Gross, "'Deutschland über Alles' and 'America First,' in Song," *New Yorker*, Feb. 18, 2017. Web.

9 James Carl Nelson, *The Polar Bear Expedition: The Heroes of America's Forgotten Invasion of Russia, 1918–1919* (New York: William Morrow, 2019).

10 Michael R. Beschloss, *Mayday: Eisenhower, Khrushchev, and the U-2 Affair* (New York: Harper and Row, 1988); Monte Reel, *A Brotherhood of Spies: The U-2 and the CIA's Secret War* (New York: Doubleday, 2018).

11 Robert J. McMahon, *The Cold War: A Very Short Introduction*, 2nd ed. (New York: Oxford University Press, 2021).

12 John Lewis Gaddis, *Strategies of Containment: A Critical Appraisal of Postwar American National Security Policy* (New York: Oxford University Press, 1982); George A. Gonzalez, *Star Trek and Star Wars: The Enlightenment versus the Anti-Enlightenment* (New York: Peter Lang, 2022), chap. 4.

even suggest that their political values, agenda were even remotely consonant with the *spirit of justice*. In the case of the American war in Vietnam the very substantial U.S. popular culture industry produced virtually no movies or television shows on the war while it was being fought (1965–1973). On its face, this indicates that the war itself was not consonant with the spirit of justice.

Nazi Cinema

The Nazi government is seemingly the most hateful regime in all of human history. As part of its hate project, the Nazis sought to deploy the modern means of communication to rally the Germany public to its skewed, myopic thinking/agenda.[13] Hitler, in *Mein Kempf*, expressed the view that one factor that led to Germany's defeat in World War I was that the Kaiser's government did a poor job on the propaganda front. Hitler was determined not to let that happen again. Joseph Goebbels, in charge of the Nazi Ministry of Propaganda, tried to use the cinema, in particular, as an instrument of political influence and control. As such, Goebbels took personal charge of movie industry and wanted the making of pro-Nazi movies. Importantly, Goebbels did not want "propaganda movies", which would only appeal to the already convinced. He wanted to naturalize (so to speak) Nazi values by embedding them in artistically appealing movies that would persuade the uninitiated.

Goebbels and the Nazis failed in their effort to make movies that unambiguously forwarded their political agenda.[14] Why? Because movies, as reflective of the *spirit of justice*, are autonomous, and not subject to the kind of instrumental control that Goebbels and the Nazis sought. Hegel would presumably consider the Nazi project a *bad infinity*—something at odds with the values of the Absolute, and this is why the Nazis never made a fictional movie that unambiguously conveyed their values and goals. In the end, the Nazis made relatively few political films and the ones that clearly aligned with the regime's political goals were not Nazi at all. Even the most notorious of Nazi fictional films, *Jud Süs*, cannot in fact be deemed anti-Semitic.

---

13 David Welch, *The Third Reich: Politics and Propaganda*, 2nd ed. (New York: Routledge, 2002); Randall L. Bytwerk, *Bending Spines: The Propagandas of Nazi Germany and the German Democratic Republic* (Lansing: Michigan State University Press, 2004); Aristotle A. Kallis, *Nazi Propaganda and the Second World War* (New York: Palgrave MacMillan, 2008).

14 Eric Rentschler, *The Ministry of Illusion: Nazi Cinema and Its Afterlife* (Cambridge, MA: Harvard University Press, 1996); Linda Schulte-Sasse, *Entertaining the Third Reich: Illusions of Wholeness in Nazi Cinema* (Durham: Duke University Press, 1996).

The Politics of Nazi Feature Films

I'll begin my treatment of Nazi films with *Jud Süs*, the most controversial and detested of all Nazi films. The reason this movie is understandably reviled has more to do with the fact we believe that the portrayal of Jews in this movie is consonant with the vile rhetoric that Hitler *et al.* directed at the Jews. Moreover, the movie can be justly viewed as a prologue to the Holocaust itself. If *Jud Süs*, however, were made in 1920 instead of 1940, we'd have a different view of it.

Certainly, *Jud Süs* has a Jewish villain—Süss Oppenheimer. But does this make it anti-Semitic? No more than having a German as a villain make a movie anti-German. Many German films did have German villains during the Nazi period. Even having a Jewish villain undercuts (to a certain extant) Nazi anti-Jewish propaganda. Süss Oppenheimer is portrayed as intelligent, capable, and charming in turns. Presumably, virtually any artistically effective protagonist must be cast in this manner. If someone is intelligent, capable and charming, aren't they by definition reformable?

Importantly, *Jud Süs* is set in 1733 and makes the point that Jews at the time were banned from a number of German cities. Presumably, the Nazis applaud this historical fact because it suggested that the German populace has always hated Jews. An honest observer (engaging the *spirit of justice*), however, would take away a different point altogether—that Jews have historically suffered terrible, completely unjust discrimination. A viewer might even conclude that Süss Oppenheimer's villainous actions are the result of such unfair treatment meted out to Jews. Additionally, while Oppenheimer plots against the well-being of the people of Swabia through his influence over the Duke of Württemberg, he is not entirely self-interested, as he convinces the Duke to allow Jews to enter the city of Stuttgart. The Jews are cast as very poor and down-trodden (to the Nazi they appear as vermin). A non-bigoted person would see humans who are in great need.

In addition to disastrously raising taxes and over-throwing the democratically elected government council, Süss Oppenheimer forces himself on a virtuous, married woman, who as a result commits suicide. For this heinous act Oppenheimer is executed. Before he is sentenced to death, Oppenheimer cravenly begs for his life. Regardless of how abjectly Oppenheimer begs for his life, in expressing love for his life the viewer can see that Oppenheimer is very human. Oppenheimer's execution can be viewed as politically motivated as he did not in fact kill anyone, but indirectly (without intending to do so) caused someone's death.

One can certainly see in *Jud Süs* Nazi hate toward Jews (in the end all Jews are again banned from Stuttgart). But if one views this movie absent any foreknowledge of the Nazis or the fact that they were behind *Jud Süs*, one would see a movie where a Jewish man does some very bad things, possibly in response to the terrible discrimination suffered by Jews. Moreover, one would become aware of the very poor conditions that Jews were historically forced to suffer. Thus, I can say with some justification that viewers of *Jud Süs* in the early 1940s were not indoctrinated into anti-Semitism because of it (*Jud Süs* was popular in German-controlled Europe), nor can this movie be viewed as a causal factor behind the Holocaust itself.

If the Nazis were unable to offer a clear-cut vilification of Jews, it's not due to a lack of desire on their part. A truly artistic film, however, seemingly cannot lend itself to the hate and demeaning of an entire people that the Nazis hoped to achieve. Presumably, this was a key factor in explaining why the Nazis made very few explicitly anti-Jewish films. Other than *Jud Süs*, the only other cinematic movie clearly intended to vilify Jews was *Die Rothchilds Aktien auf Waterloo*.[15] This movie is even further off the mark than *Jud Süs*.

In *Die Rothchilds Aktien auf Waterloo* (1940), Nathan Rothchilds (a Jew) plots and schemes to profit from the British war effort against Napoléon in the early 19th century. Significantly, Rothchilds is far from the only London-based financier seeking to profit from the British military campaign—as Rothchilds competes against other British money men who are also speculating on events surrounding the continental war. Even the Duke of Wellington himself is depicted as stealing from funds allocated to the anti-Napoléon coalition. Rothchilds, along with other British financial and military elites, place their profit-making over the well-being of the British troops and the overall war effort. Rothschilds's British financier associates treat him badly precisely because he is Jewish, which creates goodwill for Rothchilds among moviegoers. Ian Garden, who compiled an invaluable encyclopedic volume on Nazi political cinema and television, notes the irony that "the unreasonable attitude of the English bankers towards Rothchilds, simply because he is a Jew,

---

15 Ian Garden, *The Third Reich's Celluloid War: Propaganda in Nazi Feature Films, Documentaries and Television* (Gloucestershire, UK: History Press, 2015), 72–77.

actually evokes a certain sympathy and admiration from the viewer for his perseverance in the face of such adversity."[16]

Therefore, in *Die Rothchilds Aktien auf Waterloo* Goebbels *et al.* are more successful in vilifying the profit-motive than anything else. A similar conclusion can be drawn from the Nazi movie *Titanic* (1943), seemingly intended to create anti-British feelings. The movie focuses on the idea that the chief executive of the firm that owned the *Titanic* urged the captain to speed across the north Atlantic, thereby causing its tragic collision with an iceberg. A record setting voyage would have presumably raised the British company's stock, which the executive had purposively depressed to reap the rewards of Titanic's triumphant, record-setting Atlantic crossing. The first class passengers on the ship are cast in a negative light, while the lower class passengers are sympathetically treated by the film makers. Interestingly, James Cameron's very popular *Titanic* (1995) replicated all of these themes. In the end, the German version of *Titanic* denounces the fact that the chief executive (who made it onto a life boat) is exonerated by the British justice system of all wrongdoing in the sinking of *Titanic*. The implication being that wealth and power corrupted the legal proceedings.

A viewer of the movie may have a dimmer view of the British legal system by watching *Titanic*. Nevertheless, the idea that the profit motive places wealth creation above the public good as well as can cause disaster, and that the wealthy have privileged access to the justice system are critiques that can ostensibly be applied to Germany of the 1940s.

This raises the seeming fact that bias in popular culture is not found in what is depicted (as it ostensibly always demands a semblance of balance and intelligible [even reasonable] motives), but in what is not depicted. Thus, what is undoubtedly anti-Semitic about German media (including cinema) under the Nazis is not necessarily movies like *Jud Süs* or *Die Rothchilds Aktien auf Waterloo*, but in ignoring the horrific conditions that Jews endured under the Nazis. In blacking out the Holocaust (for instance) as it was happening, the public is never offered an opportunity to judge the justice or injustice of this genocide.

The Nazis came to realize that including certain (justice) motifs in their cinema could have negative political, even military, implications for them. Four German movies during the Nazi period stand out for their treatment of

---

16 Garden, *The Third Reich's Celluloid War*, 83. My treatment of Nazi films draws mostly from this highly detailed source.

imperialism: *Der Fuchs von Glenarvon* (1940); *Das Herz der Königin* (1940); *Mein Leben für Irland* (1941); and *Ohm Krüger* (1941). All were directed against the British. Nevertheless, in critically treating British imperialism in east Africa, Ireland, and South Africa, the Nazis artistically cast colonialism as implicitly predicated upon duplicity, bigotry, and violence/death/murder.[17] These movies (particularly the ones set in Ireland) were actually reported by Nazi authorities to have strengthened resistance movements in German occupied areas.[18]

Another Nazi movie that ironically reflects badly on Nazi rule is *Heimkehr* (1941), which demonizes the treatment that German-speaking minorities putatively received in Eastern Europe prior to World War Two. (The movie is set in Poland). The mistreatment of national minorities quickly invokes Nazi treatment of minorities in Germany and its occupied territories.[19]

What is perhaps most philosophically significant about cinema under the Nazis is the kind of political movies they avoided. Upon the Nazi revolution three movies expressly celebrated the Nazi party, the SA, and Hitler himself. Goebbels resisted these movies—even temporarily blocking one from release. Throughout his tenure as the chief of Nazi movies Goebbels opposed films that explicitly lauded, glorified the Nazi party and Hitler. Such hoary propaganda would convince no one and over time could even grate on rank and file Nazis.

This raises two key philosophical questions. First, why is something propaganda and not art? Second, it strongly indicates that contrary to the theorizing of the Frankfurt School concepts of justice are not malleable or instrumental, and that Staal is incorrect in asserting that hegemonic elites, groups have "control over imagination".

Therefore, viewers differentiate "art that is political" (i.e., propaganda) from "political art"—art that provides insight into politics and political phenomena.[20] Movies that would have sought to equal justice with the Nazi party and Hitler—Goebbels thought—would be ineffectual in conveying Nazi political values and convincing viewers of the justice of Nazi political goals.[21]

---

17 Garden, *The Third Reich's Celluloid War*, chap. 3.
18 Garden, *The Third Reich's Celluloid War*, 50.
19 Garden, *The Third Reich's Celluloid War*, 127.
20 Jacques Rancière, *Aesthetics and Its Discontents*, trans. Steve Corcoran (Malden, MA: Polity, 2009).
21 David Welch, *Propaganda and the German Cinema, 1933–1945* (New York: Oxford University Press, 2001), chap. 2;

Instead, Goebbels sought to place Germany's putative enemies into roles perpetrating injustice, thereby seeking to explain to viewers that they need protection from the likes of British capitalists and Jewish predators. Another evident political theme in Nazi movies is that Germans can only find justice on German soil, under the protection of the German state.[22]

Significantly, only 10 percent of the 1300 feature films made under the Nazis can be deemed political in content,[23] and only a limited number can be said to be clear-throated political tracts.[24] The fact that such a relatively small number of political movies were made under the Nazis is a testament to the inherent difficulty of adapting Nazi values and politics into satisfying art. This is especially the case because Hitler, Goebbels, and the Nazis were determined to indoctrinate the populace.[25] In the end, Goebbels and the Nazis found it easier and more politically valuable to deliver entertainment movies (comedies, adventures, suspense thrillers, etc.) to help the German public escape the drudgeries of wartime production, chronic shortages, and the bad news from the war front. Next, I take up the issue of U.S. popular culture and the American war in Vietnam.

Popular Culture and the Vietnam War

What motivated the American war in Vietnam (1965–1973)? Was it justice? Was it hate? Below I examine popular culture treatments of the American war in Vietnam. The creators of popular culture will often seek to offer the public *authentic* art, and much of the public seeks out *authentic* art. This makes

---

22 Welch, *Propaganda and the German Cinema, 1933–1945*; Siegfriend Kracauer, *From Caligari to Hitler: A Psychological History of the German Film* (Princeton: Princeton University Press, 2004 [1947]).
23 Garden, *The Third Reich's Celluloid War*, 20; also see Mary-Elizabeth Olsen, *Nazi Cinema as Entertainment: The Politics of Entertainment in the Third Reich* (Rochester, NY: Camden House, 2004).
24 Certain movies are counted as political that were mostly entertainment movies but to some significant extent touched on political ideas. Garden, *The Third Reich's Celluloid War*.
25 Jeffrey Herf, *The Jewish Enemy: Nazi Propaganda during World War II and the Holocaust* (Cambridge, MA: Belknap, 2008); Susan Bachrach, and Steven Luckert, *State of Deception: The Power of Nazi Propaganda* (Washington, DC: U.S. Holocaust Memorial Museum, 2009).

American popular culture (in its finer forms[26]) a viable source material to determine why the American war in Vietnam was fought.

After the Vietnam War was over a number of movies on the conflict were released—as was a television series. Some of these works are deemed to be anti-war. *Star Trek* (the original series), along with the movie *The Green Berets* (1968), were the only popular culture fiction (broadcast) works produced during the Vietnam War that directly commented on the conflict. Outside of Star Trek, popular culture on the Vietnam War has elided the question of justice. More precisely, (again outside of Star Trek) American popular culture on the war doesn't ask "was the goal of the American military in Vietnam justice"? While *The Green Berets* does try to engage the question of the justice of the American war against the Vietnamese communist movement, it does so, however, in a manner consistent with propaganda ("art that is political")—not "political art" (i.e., art that seeks to impart understanding of political phenomenon).[27] What might be perceived as anti-Vietnam War movies (*Apocalypse Now* [1979] and *Platoon* [1986]) are more accurately critiques of the fact that the war nearly destroyed the American military.[28] Star Trek "Private Little War" (1968) expressly holds that the war was not about justice but about geopolitical stability—"Balance of Power". Star Trek "Galileo Seven" (1967)—the creators fault the architects of the American war in Vietnam for failing to consider that the Vietnamese were motived by justice (anti-colonialism—rejecting "white supremacy"). The injustice depicted in movies like *Apocalypse Now* and *Platoon* is that U.S. soldiers died (and killed) as part of a brutal military campaign that was not about justice.

The movie *Green Berets* is propaganda because it equates justice with the U.S. The central matter in distinguishing art from propaganda is disinterestedness—creators must not appear to be advocates of any particular view of justice.[29] In the movie the audience is shown the fact that the communist movement in Vietnam is being supplied with weapons from "communist" governments. This is the reason that the U.S. is fighting in Vietnam. An

---

26 Lawrence Levine, *Highbrow/Lowbrow: The Emergence of Cultural Hierarchy in America* (Cambridge, MA: Harvard University Press, 1990).
27 Rancière, *Aesthetics and Its Discontents*.
28 Robert D. Schulzinger, *A Time for War: The United States and Vietnam, 1941–1975* (New York: Oxford University Press, 1999).
29 George A. Gonzalez, *Popular Culture as Art and Knowledge* (Lanham, MD: Lexington Books, 2019), chap. 6.

implication is that the U.S. represents justice—hence, there is no need to justify the fact that the American military is fighting/killing in Vietnam.

While there was a glaring paucity of movies on Vietnam during the war, Hollywood put out a number movies on the U.S. military and World War Two. Thus, in seeking to justify the American war in faraway Vietnam the U.S. movie industry seemingly sought to draw on the political capital that U.S. political/military institutions gained in defeating fascism in far flung regions of world.[30] The opening soliloquy to the movie *Patton* (1970) can be read as a critique (mocking) of the unquestioning belief in the U.S. military (resulting from World War Two): "That's why Americans have never lost and will never lose a war because the very thought of losing is hateful to Americans." Perhaps it's exactly this blind faith that resulted in the quagmire of Vietnam—a war with no clear military objectives.

Contrary to the fictional claim of World War Two General George S. Patton in *Patton*: "Americans traditionally love to fight. All real Americans love the sting of battle," the movie *Full Metal Jacket* (1987) indicates that American draftees had to be ceaselessly hectored and brutalized into becoming soldiers. In *Hamburger Hill* (1987) U.S. soldiers in Vietnam are profoundly weary of engaging the enemy. In the *Star Trek* (original series) episode "Day of the Dove" (1968) Captain Kirk chides those who are eager to fight solely because of the chain of command: "Be a pawn, be a toy, be a good soldier that never questions orders." *Born on the Fourth of July* (1989) is an autobiographical movie about Ron Kovic. A Vietnam veteran, Kovic comes to see his patriotic fervor for the war to be a mistake.

Why did the American military engagement in Vietnam become a quagmire? This is the subject of the movies *Apocalypse Now* and *Platoon*. What both movies are centered on is the contradictory mission of the American military in Vietnam: (1) winning hearts and minds, (2) and repressing the hostile population. *Apocalypse Now* directs overt antipathy toward the U.S. military command insofar as generals are separate from the war—safely on military bases, living in relative luxury. In *Platoon* the commanding officer of the platoon is cast as overtly incompetent and a liability to his men—killing them by sending the wrong artillery coordinates. In the *Star Trek* (original series) episode "Galileo Seven" Mr. Spock is in charge of a landing party that

---

30 Linda Dittmar, and Gene Michaud, "America's Vietnam War Films: Marching toward Denial," in *From Hanoi to Hollywood: The Vietnam War in American Film*, Linda Dittmar and Gene Michaud, eds. (New Brunswick, NJ: Rutgers University Press, 1990), chap. 1.

encounters hostile primitive natives. When natives kill members of his crew Spock is visibly indifferent to their deaths.

The focus of *Apocalypse Now* and *Platoon* is (in)stability. Both movies depict an American military that is literally falling apart in Vietnam. *Apocalypse Now* depicts a renegade officer (Colonel Kurtz) and, in general, soldiers that are undisciplined—with a riot (for instance) breaking out during a USO show featuring Playboy models. Mr. Spock's callousness in "Galileo Seven" results in ire and open insubordination. The central plot in *Platoon* is the division (Sergeant Barnes versus Sergeant Elias) that occurs within an army platoon over the killing of civilians. The result of this disagreement is soldiers murdering each other. Kurtz's has gone rogue by brutally prosecuting the war—overtly arguing this is what it takes to win. The sergeants Barnes/Elias are at odds over whether to emphasize repressing the Vietnamese or whether to focus on maintaining humane relations with them.

What those opposed to the American war effort in Vietnam see in *Apocalypse Now* and *Platoon* is the purported reality that to win the war an official policy of genocide had to be pursued—replete with Holocaust-type murder centers. Movies like *Hamburger Hill* and *Full Metal Jacket* convey the determination, ferocity with which the Vietnamese fought the U.S. military. In "Galileo Seven" the natives are determined to destroy the ship's crew. Those that support the American war effort in Vietnam, however, can see in *Apocalypse Now* and *Platoon* the critique that the military was "stabbed in the back" by leaders that prioritized politics (winning hearts) over the necessity of defeating the enemy.[31] In "Galileo Seven" Spock is urged to order the slaughter of the natives—he refuses.

In suggesting that the American military was hamstrung by political considerations and/or a misguided effort to win over the Vietnamese people *Apocalypse Now* and *Platoon* (including "Galileo Seven") ignores (even obscures) the very brutality of U.S. military policy. A scholar of American Vietnam War cinema points to the more inhumane aspects of military policy these movies elided:

> Marking free-fire zones in which any civilian was fair game; the strategic hamlet policy of forced evacuation from the destruction of ancestral villages; the defoliation of the countryside; search and destroy missions; the use of napalm, Agent Orange, and

---

31 John Marciano, *The American War in Vietnam: Crime or Commemoration?* (New York: Monthly Review, 2016); Gregory A. Daddis, *Withdrawal: Reassessing America's Final Years in Vietnam* (New York: Oxford University Press, 2017).

antipersonnel bombs; condoning rapes, torture, and mutilation of prisoners under interrogation; collecting various parts of the human anatomy as verification of kill ratios; the bombing of hospitals and schools and civilian areas of cities in North Vietnam.[32]

As noted earlier, my treatment of Nazi cinema renders the following: the bias in art is not found in what is depicted but in what is not depicted. It is telling and significant that even 50 years after the end of the Vietnam conflict, American popular culture has yet to acknowledge that the worst abuses of the American military in this conflict were directed by the high command.[33]

But again, the focus of *Apocalypse Now* and *Platoon* is not the (in)justice of the American war effort in Vietnam. Instead, these movies are centered on the stability of the American military. The creators of the television series *Tour of Duty* (1987–1990), about an American platoon in the Vietnam War, set the normative tone for the series in the pilot when the platoon leader states that the only thing that matters is the safety and cohesion (i.e., stability) of the unit. To put it more philosophically, the war fundamentally undermined the stability of a key U.S. institution—the military.

Star Trek (original series), in the episode "Private Little War", explicitly argues that the American involvement in Vietnam was about maintaining stability between the great powers of the era ("Balance of Power"). The most significant aspect of "Private Little War" I submit is that while *Green Berets* is war propaganda uncritically vaunting the American war effort in southeast Asia, this episode purportedly adopts an analytical, critical stance on U.S. involvement in Vietnam. In sharp contrast to John Wayne's lead character in *Green Berets*, Captain Kirk renders substantive (detached) commentary on the Vietnam War in "Private Little War": "do you remember the 20th century brush wars on the Asian continent?" In discussing the war Kirk finds fault with both the U.S. and the Soviet Union in using Vietnam as a battlefield in their great power competition: "Two giant powers involved ... Neither side could pull out." Kirk holds that the U.S. (along with the USSR) is involved in the "dirtiest game of them all" in Vietnam—"Balance of Power". Another original series episode, a character cynically observes (ostensibly referencing

---

32 Michael Klein, "Historical Memory, Film, and the Vietnam Era," in *From Hanoi to Hollywood: The Vietnam War in American Film*, Linda Dittmar and Gene Michaud, eds. (New Brunswick: Rutgers University Press, 1990), 28.

33 The movie *Casualties of War* (1989) depicts a scenario where military officers are indifferent to the rape and murder of a Vietnamese girl by U.S. military personnel.

the great power politics of the time): "You of the Federation, you are much like us [the Kligons].... Two tigers, predators, hunters, killers."[34] While Kirk notes that the American effort is not about justice (but stability), it is still the case that in seeking "balance" in Vietnam the U.S. engaged in wholly brutal policies. In the context of where the American military command measured success in Vietnam by the number of enemy dead,[35] Doctor McCoy's observation in "Private Little War" that "killing is stupid and useless" is a powerful, unequivocal condemnation—again, profoundly unique in American popular culture of the era.

"Galileo Seven" is a metaphorical treatment of the Vietnam War. Nevertheless, the episode is both analytical and prescient on the question of the war—given that it aired (1967) prior to the Tet Offensive (1968). *Galileo* is the name of the space shuttle that crash lands on a planet inhabited by a primitive race. The shuttle crew is led by Mister Spock. The natives manifest hostility toward the presence of *Galileo*—killing a crew member. Spock decides to intimidate the natives through a show of force—demonstrating the superiority of their weapons. Spock: "They should think twice before bothering us again.... Fear will do for us what needs to be done.... They won't attack for at least several hours."

Spock's leadership is of particular historical, philosophical importance. The character of Spock represents analytic philosophy—the idea that only material reality exists (*material realism*).[36] In a different original series episode, Spock: "I prefer the concrete, the graspable, the provable."[37] Also reflective of analytic philosophy (material realism), Spock declares in "Galileo Seven": "The sum of the parts cannot be greater than the whole." Like Spock, the U.S. government at the time of the airing of "Galileo Seven" was basing its Vietnam war effort on *the concrete, the graspable*. The *Wall Street Journal* reported in 1967 that Washington "strategists" were seeking a "victory

---

34 "Errand of Mercy" 1967——*Star Trek*, original series.
35 Harry G. Summers, "Body Count Proved to Be a False Prophet," *Los Angeles Times*, Feb. 9, 1991, A5; Gregory A. Daddis, *Westmoreland's War: Reassessing American Strategy in Vietnam* (New York: Oxford University Press, 2014).
36 Richard Hanley, *The Metaphysics of Star Trek* (New York: Basic, 1997); Nicholas Capaldi, *The Enlightenment Project in the Analytic Conversation* (Boston: Kluwer Academic Publishers, 1998); Hans-Johann Glock, *What is Analytic Philosophy?* (New York: Cambridge University Press, 2008); Stephen P. Schwartz, *A Brief History of Analytic Philosophy: From Russell to Rawls* (West Sussex, UK: Wiley-Blackwell, 2012).
37 "The Return of The Archons" 1967.

index"—"a single statistic... measuring progress" based on such metrics as enemy "casualties" (body count).[38] The U.S. government developed computer models to predict success in Vietnam using such measurable data.[39]

When despite his expectations the natives react aggressively, Spock experiences a crisis in confidence: "Most illogical reaction. We demonstrated our superior weapons. They should have fled." Faulting Spock's thought process, McCoy: "Did it ever occur to you they might react emotionally, with anger?" Spock: "I am not responsible for their unpredictability." McCoy: "They were perfectly predictable to anyone with feeling." An observer within the Kennedy/Johnson White House later critically observed that:

> The crucial factors were always the intentions of Hanoi, the will of the Viet Cong, the state of South Vietnamese politics, and the loyalties of the peasants. Not only were we deeply ignorant of these factors, but because they could never be reduced to charts and calculations, no serious effort was made to explore them.[40]

Instead, U.S. military leadership relied on "high-tech military power."[41] Spock, like American war strategists at the time, failed to consider that the desire (emotion) for justice (anti-colonialism) would overcome the Vietnamese's (native's) fear of *measurable, graspable* advanced weaponry. The Tet Offensive exposed the fallacy that American superior firepower was decisively winning the war.[42]

(In)Justice of the American War in Vietnam

Hamburger Hill indicates that the soldiers fighting the war were fully cognizant that they were not fighting for justice—or even against injustice. One soldier (indicating the lack of normative motives underlying the war): "We've been up and down this same terrain since I got here. For what?" When a soldier dies

38 "A Special Weekly Report from the Wall Street Journal's Capital Bureau," *Wall Street Journal*, Oct. 27, 1967, p. 1.
39 Alexis C. Madrigal, "The Computer That Predicted the U.S. Would Win the Vietnam War," *The Atlantic*, Oct. 5, 2017. Web.
40 As quoted in Madrigal, "The Computer That Predicted the U.S. Would Win the Vietnam War."
41 Richard N. Goodwin, *Remembering America: A Voice from the Sixties* (Boston: Little, Brown, 1988), 380.
42 James Willbanks, *The Tet Offensive: A Concise History* (New York: Colombia University Press, 2008).

in battle the sergeants in charge consciously refrain from invoking patriotism (Americanism) to make sense of the death:

> Don't tell me he died for God, country and one-hundred and first airborne...
> I'd never say that shit to anybody.

Put differently, they avoid the pitfall of *Green Berets* in equating the U.S. with justice. Worst yet, the sergeants find it offensive (even dangerous) in the context of the battlefields of the American war in Vietnam. Put differently, death for American soldiers in Vietnam is a moral waste (injustice).

Nor do the sergeants speak of the scourge of communism—something the soldiers don't mention once. Similarly, in the television series *Wonder Years* (1988–1993) episode "Walk Out" (1989) (set in 1969), when the issue of the American war in Vietnam is invoked the matter of communism is elided: "We didn't really know Ho Chi Minh from Captain Kangaroo but we knew that a lot of people were getting hurt" in the war "and we knew that it didn't seem to be doing anybody any good."

Significantly, in *Hamburger Hill* a reporter is trying to interview soldiers returning from battle—seeking chest-thumping bravado from the troops. They refuse. A sergeant tells the reporter that he has more "respect" for the enemy soldiers than for the reporter—who engages in nationalist propaganda. The soldiers are ostensibly hostile to the idea of their efforts, sacrifice being used for pro-war, pro-American agitprop: "We're gonna take this fucking hill, Newsman. I see you on the top taking pictures of any of my people I will blow your fucking head off."

Returning to the movie *Green Berets* and the issue of justice, the movie makes more of an argument about the evils of communism than the justice of America. Thus, the normative justification provided to justify the American war in Vietnam was hate—of communism (i.e., anti-communism).[43]

Conclusion

Popular culture during the Nazi period and during the American war in Vietnam is philosophically, theoretically significant—insofar there was a virtual dearth of movies, etc. that touted either Nazi values, or the "justice" of the Vietnam War. Neither of these projects were consonant with the *spirit*

---

43 Gonzalez, *Star Trek and Star Wars*, chap. 4.

of justice. This meant that movies that promoted Nazi hate or the wanton American military campaign in Vietnam couldn't be translated into *art*—other than as transparent propaganda (*The Green Berets*). Significantly, the Nazis (in their desire to make popular movies) made films that reflected badly on their project of hate, conquest, and genocide. In the context of the anti-Vietnam war movement the creators of *Star Trek* produced episodes that were sharply, pointedly critical of the war—openly acknowledging that the war was not about justice. Post-war American movies, television on the Vietnam War elided the hate (anti-communism) that was at the core of the war effort, and tended to focus on the issue of stability—the argument that the war de-stabilized the American military. Justice in these movies is in the negative—the injustice of the death of U.S. soldiers in a war that arguably appeared senseless to the soldiers themselves.

· 3 ·

THE PROGRESSIVE POLITICS OF 1950S SCI-FI MOVIES AND STAR TREK OF THE 1960S

During the 1950s a bevy of *outer space* related sci-fi movies were produced in the United States.[1] Robert P. Kolker, in *Triumph over Containment: American Film in the 1950s*, holds that the science fiction genre of the era is of a piece with the anti-communism of the times.[2] Kolker points to the dominant themes of 1950s sci-fi cinema: dangerous aliens and dark conspiracies. He specifically avers that "technologies of destruction and alien ideologies were planted in the minds of postwar Americans, and they were frightened."[3] Anti-communism is the idea of the monolith of global communism/communists—a sinister, dastardly, disciplined unitary movement not to be reasoned with.[4] In contradistinction to Kolker, I argue that the most productive foreground to use in analyzing the sci-fi movies of the 1950s is the Enlightenment (technological optimism; secularism; globalism)—not the hate of anti-communism. The

---

1 John Wade, *The Golden Age of Science Fiction: A Journey into Space with 1950s Radio, TV, Films, Comics and Books* (Barnsley, UK: Pen and Sword History, 2019).
2 Robert P. Kolker, *Triumph over Containment: American Film in the 1950s* (New Brunswick, NJ: Rutgers University Press, 2022), chap. 6.
3 Kolker, *Triumph over Containment*, 108.
4 David M. Oshinsky, *A Conspiracy So Immense: The World of Joe McCarthy* (New York: Oxford University Press, 2005).

progressivism of 1950s sci-fi movies is brought into sharp relief through comparison with the sci-fi television series *Star Trek* that aired in the late 1960s.

The Enlightenment and *Outer Space* Popular Culture

Gene Roddenberry, the prime creative force behind *Star Trek*, was determined to use the Enlightenment features of outer space-oriented popular culture[5] to produce an artwork squarely centered on universal justice, fairness. Roddenberry "believed that a peaceful, harmonious, unified Earth must be the result of a natural and logical evolution of society."[6] Writing in 1976, Roddenberry explained that "the optimistic point we did make is that [in the world of *Star Trek*] mankind finally learned the foolishness of petty nationalism and political and racial hatreds and finally discarded them. There was no USA in our series."[7] The movie creators of the 1950s were operating in the repressive milieu of rising anti-Soviet fervor and the McCarthyite witch-hunt,[8] whereas *Star Trek* was made in the context of the anti-Vietnam war movement, as well as the civil rights and feminist movements.[9]

Nevertheless, the very notion of space travel (conveyed in 1950s sci-fi films) bespeaks an optimism in science and technology—the Enlightenment.[10] The 1950 movie, *Destination Moon*, communicates humanity's determined commitment to go into space—even when government decides against it.

---

5 David Seed, *Science Fiction: A Very Short Introduction* (New York: Oxford University Press, 2011); Russell Blackford, *Science Fiction and the Moral Imagination: Visions, Minds, Ethics* (Cham, DEN: Springer Publishing, 2017).
6 Stephen E. Whitfield, with Gene Roddenberry, *The Making of Star Trek* (New York: Ballantine Books, 1968), 112.
7 As quoted in David Alexander, *Star Trek Creator: The Authorized Biography of Gene Roddenberry* (New York: Penguin Books, 1994), 421.
8 Patrick McGilligan, and Paul Buhle, *Tender Comrades: A Backstory of the Hollywood Blacklist* (New York: St. Martin's Press, 1997).
9 Editors of LIFE, *LIFE The 1960s: The Decade When Everything Changed* (New York: LIFE, 2016); Henry Finder, ed., *The 60s: The Story of a Decade* (New York: New Yorker, 2016); Editors of History Channel, *History The 1960's* (New York: History Channel, 2019).
10 Jonathan I. Israel, *Radical Enlightenment: Philosophy and the Making of Modernity, 1650–1750* (New York: Oxford University Press, 2001), *Enlightenment Contested: Philosophy, Modernity, and the Emancipation of Man, 1670–1752* (New York: Oxford University Press, 2006), and *The Expanding Blaze: How the American Revolution Ignited the World, 1775–1848* (Princeton: Princeton University Press, 2017).

When the U.S. government opts to suspend its program to reach the moon, private individuals and capital are mobilized to achieve this momentous (technologically challenging) goal.[11] Aliens, even when hostile (the space monsters of 1950s sci-fi movies), are a reflection of secularism—the idea that intelligent life (humanity) is not the creation of a deity, but the result of an evolutionary process that in all likelihood occurred on planets other than Earth. In *Star Trek* humanity has mastered space travel—reaching the farthest reaches of the galaxy, and is part of an interstellar organization (the Federation) that incorporates numerous alien planets/intelligent species.

Sci-Fi and Anti-Communism

On the issue of anti-communism itself, it makes an explicit sci-fi appearance only in the negative (criticism of it). *Star Trek* episode "Day of the Dove" (1968)—an alien is surreptitiously prompting animosity between the Enterprise crew and Klingons on board—Kirk rhetorically asks: "Has a war been staged for us, complete with... *ideology* [anti-communism] and patriotic drum beating?" What we don't see in the movies that Kolker critiques as reflecting anti-communism are "communists" nor the Soviet Union as villains. At a minimum, the sci-fi movies of the 1950s didn't directly contribute to the political tensions of the Cold War.

The *Invasion of the Body Snatchers* (1956) is, according to Kolker, "the most potent of '50s alien invasion films"—holding that the film is pro-McCarthyite witch-hunt artwork as it warns against "Communist thought control" (quoting J. Edgar Hoover—arch anti-communist and longtime head of the FBI).[12] Other 1950s sci-fi movies that use mind control as plot device are *Invaders from Mars* (1953) and *It Came from Outer Space* (1953). If viewers, however, read a politics into the alien mind control trope of these movies, it is anti-communists that sought to *control thought*—promoting mindless hate (the fiction of anti-communism). *Star Trek* "Day of the Dove"—the action begins when the Enterprise rescues the crew from a Klingon vessel as it explodes.

---

11 Kolker suggests that the reliance on private capital to finance the trip to the moon is pro-capitalist. Importantly, however, the motive behind the trip is not profit. *Triumph over Containment*, 109-110.

12 Kolker, *Triumph over Containment*, 123. Also see Steven M. Sanders, "Interpreting *Invasion of the Body Snatchers*," in *The Philosophy of Science Fiction Film*, Steven M. Sander, ed. (Lexington: University of Kentucky Press, 2008).

The Enterprise crew and the Klingons engage in hostilities—with hate, anger and false accusations emanating from both sides. They are being psychologically manipulated (mentally controlled) to hate each other by an alien entity that literally consumes emotions and specifically "exists on the hate of others." Optimistically, in the end, the Klingons and the Enterprise crew come together to vanquish the alien fostering the hostilities. To the alien: "Maybe you've caused a lot of suffering, a lot of history, but that's all over."

This is ostensibly a direct, full-throated rejection of anti-communist factions within the U.S. Nick Fischer, in *Spider Web: The Birth of American Anticommunism*, outlines how a network of individuals strategically situated within the U.S. polity (including the media) perennially/publicly engaged in hate-mongering against what it deemed *communism* and *communists*.[13] A prominent, central member of this network was Hoover, who would consistently emphasize the national security, and the domestic political, threat of communism—thereby fostering a milieu of fear, hate, and hysteria.[14] This anti-communist network would smear dissenters of all stripes as "communist dupes" and *un-American*—including those that advocated for a policy of peaceful co-existence with the USSR.[15]

A subtle, yet powerful critique of anti-communism is found in *Star Trek*—"Patterns of Force" (1968). This episode portrays a Nazi regime on the planet of Ekos. With Nazism as the political basis of Ekos, the Ekosians organize around the vilification of Zeons—a population from a neighboring planet. The Nazi regime organizes a planned genocide ("Their Final Solution") against the Zeons. The idea that U.S. anti-communism is picking up the baton from the Nazis on the question of the Soviet Union can be read into "Patterns of Force". ("Why do the Nazis hate Zeons?" "Because without us to hate, there'd be nothing to hold them together.") The hate of communism/communists (i.e., anti-communism) was deployed to unite the American public in fighting the Cold War.

Anti-communism can be categorized as *bullshit*—per Harry Frankfurt. Frankfurt argues that in the modern context something he labels "bullshit" has been created—a new category of epistemology (knowledge).[16] Bullshit is a completely false narrative—entirely disconnected from history, facts. The

---

13 Nick Fischer, *Spider Web: The Birth of American Anticommunism* (Urbana: University of Illinois Press, 2016).
14 Curt Gentry, *J. Edgar Hoover: The Man and the Secrets* (New York: Norton, 2001).
15 Oshinsky, *A Conspiracy So Immense*.
16 Harry G. Frankfurt, *On Bullshit* (Princeton: Princeton University Press, 2005).

Nazis were seemingly the first to engage in a policy, politics of Bullshit with their Big Lie technique—the repeating (through modern means of communication) of politically motivated fantasies over and over again (the Aryan Race, the Jewish Conspiracy, etc.). The false construct/specter of Iraq's WMDs (weapons of mass destruction) allowed the George W. Bush administration, with the help of the *New York Times* and other national/international media, to invade Iraq in 2003.[17]

Roughly 40 years prior to Frankfurt's book *On Bullshit*, this mode of anti-epistemology was identified in *Star Trek* as representing a kind of mind control. Part of the anti-Klingon hysteria in "Day of the Dove" was the earlier killing of the brother of an Enterprise officer (Chekov). Chekov is myopically hate-filled. He denounces the Klingons as "filthy... monsters" because they slaughtered his brother "Piotre." It turns out that Chekov "never had a brother. He's an only child." The hate mongering alien in "Day of the Dove" is impelling Chekov through *bullshit*—a false narrative that had no relationship to reality. As alluded to above, an obvious example of bullshit in the context of the Cold War was the insistence on the monolith of (sinister) global communism/communists.[18]

Another *Star Trek* (original series) episode also engages the issue of mind control: "The Return of the Archons" (1967), but in this case critiquing political religion (theocracy)—with the anti-communist turn of the 1950s embracing politically conservative Christianity.[19] The episode focuses on a planet where a religious cult predominates—centered on the figure of "Landru". The religion of Landru is described as retrograde, as under this religion society went "back to a simple time." The planet's society was technologically advanced but it returned to 19th century small-town life, and has been in this state for 6000 years.

Kirk decides to destroy the machine that imposes the cult of Landru, and in so doing expressly holds that because of this religion this society is not "a

---

17 James Ryerson, "Harry G. Frankfurt, a Philosopher Eager to Cut the Bull, Dies at 94," *New York Times*, July 18, 2023, A17.
18 Oshinsky, *A Conspiracy So Immense*.
19 Michael Graziano, *Errand Into the Wilderness of Mirrors*: Religion and the History of the CIA (Chicago: University of Chicago Press, 2021); Carl R. Weinberg, *Red Dynamite: Creationism, Culture Wars, and Anticommunism in America* (Ithaca: Cornell University Press, 2021); Lerone A. Martin, *The Gospel of J. Edgar Hoover: How the FBI Aided and Abetted the Rise of White Christian Nationalism* (Princeton: Princeton University Press, 2023).

living, growing culture." Directly implying that political religion stifles autonomous thought and a vibrant, evolving society, Kirk (to the computer that upholds the cult of Landru): "Without creativity, there is no life. The body [i.e., community] dies." Spock adds: "Creativity is necessary for the health of the Body."

Invasion of the Body Snatchers is about more than mind control. In this film alien created replicas replace people (taking over their persona), and the replicas are zombie-like, mindless. This mirrors the radical shift that took place in American politics during the 1950s. The 1930s and 1940s (the New Deal) was a time of social justice, progressivism, and friendship with the Soviet Union.[20] Political leaders, the media did a decisive (almost inexplicable) about face in the 1950s[21]—with anti-capitalism; a pro-Soviet stance; and demands for gender, ethnic equality officially denounced as impermissible (*communist*) treachery.[22] It's like replicas literally took over people's persona. The very individuals, institutions that had a critical sensibility in the 1930s and 1940s now in the 1950s actively imposed the hate, irrationality, repression of anti-communism. A salient example of someone who went from a New Deal adherent (expressing admiration for FDR) to a strident anti-communist Cold War warrior was Ronald Reagan.[23]

In *Star Trek* the suggestion is made that in the context of the Cold War the U.S. had forgotten its values (McCarthyism). In "The Omega Glory" (1968) the Enterprise crew encounters a planet identical to Earth except the Cold War resulted in a nuclear/biological weapons conflagration—reducing the population to a veritable stone age. The "Yangs" (representing the West) worships the American Constitution (the document), but it has no specific meaning for them (i.e., they are unable to read it). Ultimately, (as outlined in Chapter 5) Kirk reminds them of the values that had informed America. Episode "Court Martial" (1967)—the following was a salient critique in the aftermath of the McCarthyite witch-hunt of the 1950s and early 1960s,

---

20 Eric Rauchway, *The Great Depression and the New Deal: A Very Short Introduction* (New York: Oxford University Press, 2009).
21 Robert J. McMahon, *The Cold War: A Very Short Introduction*, 2nd ed. (New York: Oxford University Press, 2021).
22 William T. Walker, *McCarthyism and the Red Scare: A Reference Guide* (Santa Barbara, CA: ABC-CLIO, 2011); Jonathan Michaels, *McCarthyism: The Realities, Delusions and Politics Behind the 1950s Red Scare* (New York: Routledge, 2017).
23 Edward M. Yager, *Ronald Reagan's Journey: Democrat to Republican* (Lanham, MD: Rowman & Littlefield, 2006).

where people's careers, lives were destroyed on the basis of innuendo, gossip, and secret testimony:[24] "Rights, sir, human rights. The Bible, the Code of Hammurabi and of Justinian, Magna Carta, the Constitution of the United States... these documents all speak of rights... most importantly, the right to be confronted by the witnesses against him."

Globalism

Arguably, the most politically progressive aspects of 1950s sci-fi films is their implied or explicit globalism—issues facing not the nation, but the planet. With the defeat of fascism, and with the New Deal and Soviet "socialism" combating poverty and other social ills, the popular imagination turned to the "Final Frontier" (a phrase popularized with *Star Trek*). Movie makers in the 1950s opted in many/most cases to focus on the potential (imagined, fantasy) dangers of outer space (monsters).

The creators of *Star Trek* are optimist about space exploration insofar as they expressly link it to social, economic progress (universal justice). They do so in the episode "City on the Edge of Forever" (1967)—set during Depression Era (1930s) New York City. One, Edith Keeler, speechifies optimistically to a group of homeless about a future without poverty, where all can thrive: "The men that reach out into space will be able to find ways to feed the hungry millions of the world and to cure their diseases. They will be able to find a way to give each man hope and a common future." A vision (of technological advancement serving the ends of social justice) is consonant with FDR's New Deal[25]—Roosevelt being reverentially invoked in the episode.

The Day the Earth Stood Still (1951) is explicitly a rejection of anti-communism ("unreasoning suspicions and attitudes") and an argument for globalism—even global government. The alien protagonist holds that now that humanity has the power of atomic weapons that it must live "in peace or... face obliteration." The idea that technology is outpacing humanity's ability to safely manage it is made by Captain Kirk in the fictional 23rd century

24 Rebecca Prime, *Hollywood Exiles in Europe: The Blacklist and Cold War Film Culture* (New Brunswick, NJ: Rutgers University Press, 2014); Christopher M. Elias, *Gossip Men: J. Edgar Hoover, Joe McCarthy, Roy Cohn, and the Politics of Insinuation* (Chicago: University of Chicago Press, 2021).

25 Kiran Klaus Patel, *The New Deal: A Global History* (Princeton: Princeton University Press, 2016); Kenneth J. Bindas, *Modernity and the Great Depression: The Transformation of American Society, 1930–1941* (Lawrence: University Press of Kansas, 2017).

(ostensibly referencing the Cold War—e.g., the Cuban Missile Crisis): "There came a time when our weapons grew faster than our wisdom, and we almost destroyed ourselves" (*Star Trek*—"Private Little War" 1968). As noted above, in "The Omega Glory" the Enterprise crew encounters a planet identical to Earth except the Cold War resulted in a nuclear/biological weapons conflagration.

In *The Day the Earth Stood Still* other worlds are prepared to destroy the planet because they fear that humanity's intra-planetary warmongering and political tensions pose a broader threat—now that humans control nuclear weapons. Thus, humans should shift their focus from the geo-politics of Earth's nation-states to that of interstellar space—as the direct threat is from other planets. While less cerebral, the same conclusion about reorienting humanity's geo-political attention can be drawn from *War of the Worlds* (1953)—as Earth is invaded by an alien military force.

The animated DC Comics movie, *Justice League: The New Frontier* (2008), set in the 1950s reprises the dangerous alien genre of the period. In the face of a powerful entity determined to eliminate humanity because humans are destroying the environment, Superman calls for solidarity (arguably globalism)—i.e., the setting aside of political differences: "All of you remember... today there are no Democrats, no Republicans... no hawks, no doves. Just the naked simplicity of an absolute: mankind's survival." Notably, the creators of this Justice League movie critically comment on the politics of the 1950s: U.S. foreign policy, McCarthyism, and the political violence of the South. In the case of foreign policy, reflecting the fact that the U.S. was supporting the "Indo-China" counter-insurgency campaign in "1954" Wonder Women oversees the massacre of unarmed insurgents—defending this action (unironically) as "the American Way". Superman *et al.* are pressed into signing "loyalty oaths". Senator Joseph McCarthy is referred to as a "boogeyman". Rejecting McCarthysm, Superman holds "We need our heroes to stand up and show us what this country is suppose to mean." Commenting on U.S. politics in the 1950s (ostensibly anti-communism), an alien from Mars (who has been living in America) observes that "There's too much hate here... too much ignorance... too much mindless conformity." The audience is told through a television news report that someone named "Wilson" worked to protect people in the South from "white supremacists", but he "was caught by a mob and killed." Pointing to the complicity of the police in such killings (lynchings), the news report contains the following: "Police say they have no suspects." (See Chapter 4 for a treatment of Southern racism and political violence.)

In the world of *Star Trek*, Earth is unified and part of the Federation, an interstellar institution. A statement of global solidarity is expressed by Kirk and Spock (a Vulcan) in "Whom Gods Destroy" (1969). Kirk speaks of the founders of the Federation: "They had a dream. A dream that... spread throughout the stars. A dream that made Mister Spock and me brothers." Indicative of how the Federation transcends all political identities, Spock, when asked if he considers Captain Kirk a "brother" responds: "What he says is logical and I do, in fact, agree with it."

A similar point of global solidarity is made in the Star Trek episode "Court Martial". Captain Kirk is tried by a multi-ethnic panel of four officers—one member with an Afro background and another with a central Asian background. (Kirk—based on doctored evidence—is wrongly accused of negligence in the death of an officer.) At the opening of the proceedings, Kirk is asked "if you feel that any of these [individuals] harbor any prejudiced attitudes to your case"?—as Kirk has the "right to ask for substitute officers." Kirk: "I have no objections"—firmly believing that ethnicity (nor gender—a female prosecutor) will have any bearing whatsoever on the trial that will determine his fate.

"Mirror, Mirror" (1967) arguably provides a critique of American political, military global machinations. Members of Enterprise crew are inadvertently transported to an alternate universe. The Enterprise exists in this alternate universe, but instead of the Federation the political authority is the "Empire"—where "behavior and discipline" is "brutal, savage." Kirk is "ordered to annihilate the Halkans unless they comply [and give their energy deposits to the Empire]. *No alternative*"—whereas in the Federation universe the Enterprise only pursued peaceful means with the Halkans. "Mirror, Mirror" is an explicit rejection/critique of military intervention into other societies—particularly for purposes of controlling natural resources. A censure that can be issued to the U.S. of the Cold War Era.

Seemingly, the sci-fi popular culture most explicitly about global politics is the film *The Red Planet Mars* (1952). When people believe that a utopian civilization on Mars has been discovered, this creates upheaval throughout the world, as well as dramatic political shifts (in the USSR—improbably its leadership becomes devoutly religious). This reflects the reality that in the modern era events in one country have globally (decisively) changed politics. The American Revolution (1775–1783), with its motto "All Men are Created

Equal", was a precursor to the anti-aristocratic French Revolution (1789),[26] which, itself, profoundly changed European politics.[27]

A global politics is depicted in the *Star Trek* episode "Savage Curtain" (1969)—which features Abraham Lincoln as a character. Lincoln comes to life in "Savage Curtain" because an alien race wants to learn about good and evil—ideas that are foreign to them. The aliens create figures from the past— Lincoln being one of them. The camps designated "good" and "evil" ultimately fight it out in an experiment to learn about these concepts. Lincoln is in the camp representing good. While Lincoln was an American President, as the leader of the Northern victory over the Southern slavocracy he is a figure of worldwide saliency—defeating feudalism in the West, and the concomitant triumph of progressive modernism.[28] The point is made in the edited volume *The Global Lincoln* that Abraham Lincoln's "global celebrity lies in... his resolute defense of popular government and free labor."[29]

Of the avatars created to conduct the alien's experiment, Lincoln (by far) receives the most attention—as he is a guest abroad Enterprise (whereas the others are not). Significantly, James T. Kirk (captain of the Enterprise) in the 23rd century strongly admires the personage of Lincoln, so much so that Kirk shows great deference and respect to what is obviously an ersatz Lincoln.[30] The fact that Kirk (and others) would admire Lincoln 300 years after his death and in a context of world government (i.e., the U.S. no longer exists) in-and-itself indicates that Lincoln is a figure of substantial historic and global importance.

Importantly, other than Lincoln on the "good" team is Surak—a Vulcan. He is cast as a modernizing figure for the Vulcans. Spock on Surak: "The greatest of all who ever lived on our planet, Captain. The father of all we became." Hence, Lincoln and Surak (who are teamed together along with

---

26   Israel, *The Expanding Blaze: How the American Revolution Ignited the World, 1775–1848*.

27   Jeremy D. Popkin, *A New World Begins: The History of the French Revolution* (New York: Basic Books, 2019); William Doyle, *The French Revolution: A Very Short Introduction*, 2nd ed. (New York: Oxford University Press, 2020).

28   Roland Vegso, *The Naked Communist: Cold War Modernism and the Politics of Popular Culture* (New York: Fordham University Press, 2013). Modernism is a set of normative values that privileges reason and secularism, as opposed to obscurantism and political religion (i.e., theocracy). Peter Childs, *Modernism*, 3rd ed. (New York: Routledge, 2016).

29   Richard Carwardine and Jay Sexton, eds., *The Global Lincoln* (New York: Oxford University Press, 2011), ix

30   James M. McPherson, *Abraham Lincoln and the Second American Revolution* (New York: Oxford University Press, 1992); James Oakes, *Freedom National: The Destruction of Slavery in the United States* (New York: W.W. Norton & Company, 2012).

Kirk and Spock) mirror each other—as both were world changing figures for their planets. The ersatz Surak, when first meeting humans, responds in a globalist, universalist manner: "In my time, we knew not of Earth men. I am pleased to see that we have differences. May we together become greater than the sum of both of us."

Conclusion

Kolker asserts that the sci-fi movies of the 1950s reflect anti-communist themes, motifs. Viewers today watching these movies would have little reason to see the Cold War (anti-communism) in them. The salient tropes in these films of mind control and alien created replicas (far from communicating anti-communist biases) can most readily be read as critiques of anti-communism, anti-communists—as expressly conveyed in the *Star Trek* episodes "Day of the Dove" and "The Return of the Archons". It would not be until the 1960s—"Omega Glory" and "Court Martial"—that a sci-fi admonishment would be put forward critiquing the fact that in the 1950s America abandoned its Constitutional principles.

The outer space films of the 1950s are predicated on the Enlightenment (technological optimism, evolution), the social justice politics of the New Deal as well as Soviet "socialism", and the globalism of the world-wide struggle against fascism. People believed that the next logical objective of humanity was exploring space. The fact that many film makers in the 1950s chose to focus on the (fantasy) perils of outer space does not make such movies anti-communist propaganda. Moreover, *The Day the Earth Stood Still* is an unambiguously progressive film—expressly rejecting anti-communism and arguing for the necessity of global solidarity in the nuclear age. Founded on the putative reality of globalist politics is *The Red Planet Mars*—where a salient event (the discovery of a utopian society on Mars) affects the entirety of Earth's nation-states' politics. *Star Trek* in the 1960s would fully embrace, depict the Enlightenment outlook and globalism of the *outer space* sci-fi genre.

· 4 ·

STAR TREK (ORIGINAL SERIES) AT THE CENTER OF THE JUSTICE (VALUES) REVOLUTION OF THE 1960S

The 1950s was a particularly repressive period in U.S. history. This was the height of the anti-communist hysteria.[1] With anti-communism came a resurgence of white supremacy[2] and rigid patriarchy.[3] As a result (along with the repression of dissent), minorities suffered greatly—women, gays, lesbians, African Americans, etc. experienced dramatic setbacks. The regressiveness of this period is arguably most emblematic with the television series *Father Knows Best* (1954–1960). The overt implication is that the official family of the U.S. (at the height of its global power) is white; unquestioning of corporate or American power; heterosexual; with the male (father) as head of household.[4] The father is due the deference of the family—who will represent the family in

---

1 David M. Oshinsky, *A Conspiracy So Immense: The World of Joe McCarthy* (New York: Oxford University Press, 2005); Christopher M. Elias, *Gossip Men: J. Edgar Hoover, Joe McCarthy, Roy Cohn, and the Politics of Insinuation* (Chicago: University of Chicago Press, 2021).
2 Editorial Board, "Why Does the U.S. Military Celebrate White Supremacy?" *New York Times*, May 24, 2020, SR8.
3 Gerda Lerner, *The Creation of Patriarchy* (New York: Oxford University Press, 1986).
4 The U.S. Department of Treasury commissioned in 1959 an episode of *Father Knows Best* as an expressed piece of propaganda—titled "24 Hours in Tyrant Land." Tim Brooks and

the public sphere and select the life course of his children (remember, Father Knows Best!). The duty of women is to marry, have and nurture children, and, importantly, submit to her husband's authority (as well as uphold it).[5]

My argument in this chapter is that the *Star Trek* television series of the 1960s presented a uniquely strong stance in favor of justice—denouncing the discrimination and oppression that women and African Americans experienced during this period. Thus, the creators of *Star Trek* were not simply conveying, commenting on the politics of its day, they were direct participants in advocating for justice/fairness. *Star Trek* episodes "Elaan of Troyius" (1968) and "Turnabout Intruder" (1969) present female characters openly, unambiguously, stridently railing against the sexism of the times. Moreover, Star Trek presented a future with a world government, and total ethnic equality—including the hero worship of Abraham Lincoln (episode "Savage Curtain" [1969]). "Let that Be your Last Battlefield" (1969) directly critiques the racial hate of the Jim Crow South. The use of racism to prop up a profoundly unjust social order is depicted in "The Cloud Minders" (1969) and the creators of "Day of the Dove" (1968) denounce the use of racism by anti-communists. I begin the analysis by outlining the anti-sexism of original series *Star Trek*, and follow this by describing its anti-racism.

Star Trek as Feminist Tract

The liberal feminist[6] movement of the 1960s helped undue much of the repression that women experienced in the 1950s.[7] *Star Trek* can be deemed as a salient part of this movement as it is distinct from what can be deemed feminist television in the late 1960s and early 1970s. Shows like *Julia* (1968–1971) and *Mary Tyler Moore* (1970–1977) depict single women successfully making

---

Earle Marsh, *The Complete Directory to Prime Time Network and Cable TV Shows 1946–Present* (Twentieth Anniversary ed.) (New York: Ballantine Books, 1999), 338.

5 Marilyn Yalom, *A History of the Wife* (New York: HarperCollins, 2001); Stephanie Coontz, *Marriage, a History: From Obedience to Intimacy, or How Love Conquered Marriage* (New York: Viking, 2005); Lauren Jae Gutterman, *Her Neighbor's Wife: A History of Lesbian Desire within Marriage* (Philadelphia: University of Pennsylvania Press, 2020).

6 Kimberly Wilmot Voss, *Women Politicking Politely: Advancing Feminism in the 1960s and 1970s* (Lanham, MD: Lexington Books, 2017).

7 Editors of LIFE, *LIFE The 1960s: The Decade When Everything Changed* (New York: LIFE, 2016); Henry Finder, ed., *The 60s: The Story of a Decade* (New York: New Yorker, 2016); Editors of History Channel, *History The 1960's* (New York: History Channel, 2019).

their way in the world, but they stayed clear of bemoaning the systematic, debilitating, frustrating discrimination (oppression) that women faced.[8] *Star Trek* stands out on this score.

David Greven holds that the bold progressiveness of *Star Trek* (original series) in the realms of gender and queer politics is that marriage and biological family play only a minimal role in the series.[9] Instead, *Star Trek* features individuals that find meaningful fellowship, emotional intimacy among co-workers, friends. On the question of gender, the regular character of Lt. Uhura is noteworthy—she's a career woman and a bridge officer. With regard to homosexuality, *Star Trek* of the 1960s had no gay or lesbian characters, but, significantly, the series had what can be deemed the gayest moment of American television (certainly up until that time). In "Turnabout Intruder" (described in more detail below) Captain Kirk's body is taken over by a woman. Her/his co-conspirator is a male, who she apparently manipulated with sex. While in Kirk's body, this character uses her feminine charms on her accomplice—pulling up behind him, gently placing his hand on his shoulder, and speaking to him in a seductive tone. He complies with her/his request.

Women as Strong

Daniel Leonard Bernardi, in *Star Trek and History: Race-ing toward a White Future*, takes an ahistorical tack and denounces the fact that the character of Lt. Uhura was a supporting role.[10] The disparaging of the Uhura character ignores the great importance of having a bridge officer on the Enterprise in the late 1960s that is a female (and African American). Regardless of the content of the role, the character of Uhura on the bridge of the Enterprise week in and week out glaringly communicated that the future of humanity was one of ethnic, gender equality.

Moreover, women in the original series play autonomous, assertive characters—including that of a Romulan ship captain, who has male

---

8 Josh Ozersky, *Archie Bunker's America: TV in an Era of Change, 1968-1978* (Carbondale: Southern Illinois University Press, 2003); Judy Kutulas, *After Aquarius Dawned: How the Revolutions of the Sixties became the Popular Culture of the Seventies* (Chapel Hill: University of North Carolina Press, 2017), chap. 3.

9 David Greven, *Gender and Sexuality in Star Trek: Allegories of Desire in the Television Series and Films* (Jefferson, NC: MacFarland, 2009).

10 Daniel Leonard Bernardi, *Star Trek and History: Race-ing toward a White Future* (New Brunswick, NJ: Rutgers University Press, 1998).

subordinates ("The Enterprise Incident" 1968). "Time Amok" (1967) has Mr. Spock's betrothed scheming to escape their arranged marriage. A young woman in "Cloud Minders" eschews a life of comfort and opulence to live among the poor, destitute of her planet. "Day of the Dove" features a woman as a Klingon science officer, who breaks with her commanding officer (also her husband)—holding that Kirk *et al.* possess the correct understanding of the situation facing both the Klingon and Enterprise crews. The Elaan, Dohlman of Elas, is an (aristocratic) political leader—the men in her entourage kneel before her. She prioritizes strategic thinking: "We are interested in how the ship is used in combat, not in what drives it. Engines are for mechanics and menials" ("Elaan of Troyius"). "Wink of an Eye" (1968) features a woman leader of a group seeking to take over the Enterprise. She asserts her sexuality—kissing Captain Kirk (trying to seduce him) and calling him "pretty." Similarly, Elaan tells Captain Kirk "I chose you." "Court Martial" (1967) has a female lead prosecutor.

The character of Edith Keeler in "City on the Edge of Forever" (1967) is particularly significant as a feminist figure in the later 1960s. Greven, in his outstanding book *Gender and Sexuality in Star Trek*, makes the effective argument that Kirk's trysts were mostly cast as exotic and extraneous.[11] The one exception to this is Kirk's relationship with Keeler. She has committed her life to helping the poor, dispossessed—overseeing the "21st Street Mission". In the context of Great Depression 1930s New York, Keeler's kindness, charity, and idealism render her endearing, attractive to the audience as a well as to Kirk. Kirk and Keeler share the same social justice values of the 1960s counterculture (including an anti-war outlook):

> Keeler: I think that one day they'll take all the money they spend now on war and death
> Kirk: And make them spend it on life?
> Keeler: Yes. You see the same things that I do. We speak the same language.
> Kirk: The very same.

As noted in Chapter 3, Keeler speechifies optimistically about a future of justice—without poverty, where all can thrive. Keeler's autonomy, leadership, and political awareness makes her an iconic figure of 1960s feminism—especially considering the countless times that the episode "City on the Edge of Forever" has been broadcast around the world.

---

11 Greven, *Gender and Sexuality in Star Trek*.

Women as Second Class Citizens

Importantly, while positing an image of women as autonomous and assertive, *Star Trek* directly confronts the hardships that they endure. For instance, unlike men, women at the time had to mostly choose between career or family. "The Man Trap" (1966) did feature a husband-and-wife archaeological team, but, conversely, Lt. Uhura is unmarried and childless. Episode "Is There In Truth No Beauty?" (1968) centers on a female character who places career above romantic entanglement. When she refuses her suitor, he chides her by questioning her womanhood: "Why don't you try being a woman for a change?" Captain Kirk's former lover rebukes him for choosing Starfleet over a relationship with her. He indicates that she's too strong willed: "We'd have killed each other" ("Turnabout Intruder").

Elaan, Dohlman of Elas, is a metaphor for the pressure that women face to marry, and that they're expected to demure to their husbands (i.e., to be ladylike) ("Elaan of Troyius"). She is livid that she's being forced to marry the ruler of Troyius. The Ambassador of Troyius: "Our two warring planets now possess the capability of mutual destruction. Some method of co-existence must be found." Elaan: "I will never forgive the council for putting me through this torture." She brutally stabs the Ambassador of Troyius because he expected that she "adopt... servile manners"—that is, conform to traditional female etiquette. Elaan ruefully notes: "That's all you men... can speak of, duty and responsibility." She concludes that as a woman "I have only responsibilities and obligations," and, conversely, no freedom—as she's being forced to marry and kowtow to her husband.

Captain Kirk (in response to Elaan's obstreperous behavior): "Mister Spock, the women on your planet are logical. That's the only planet in this galaxy that can make that claim." Of course, this claim can be read as sexist. A broader read is that women shouldn't be pigeonholed into the institution of marriage. Women, like men, are inherently unpredictable (that is, illogical), each with their own unique hopes, dreams, aspirations. Nor should women be forced into traditional female etiquette—which demands a woman be genteel, demure.[12] Women are especially expected to be emotionally self-contained, reserved in public.[13] "Logic" for men and women is different, and

---

12 Kim E. Nielsen, *Money, Marriage, and Madness: The Life of Anna Ott* (Urbana: University of Illinois Press, 2020).
13 Laura Claridge, *Emily Post: Daughter of the Gilded Age, Mistress of American Manners* (New York: Random House, 2009); Ted Ownby, ed., *Manners and Southern History* (Jackson: University Press of Mississippi, 2011).

skewed against women openly (unabashedly) expressing anger, displeasure, desire, ambition, etc. Elann (with her "illogical" behavior)—angry shouting; making unreasonable demands; acting out by breaking objects—is an ironic metaphor of the oppressive strictures that women have to endure.

The creators of *Star Trek* take specific aim at the conservative (mis)treatment of women. A metaphor for Saudi Arabia is depicted in "Friday's Child" (1967)—while not veiled, the women dress in the manner redolent of the traditional Middle East. The planet Capella Four is governed by the Ten Tribes and a rigid patriarchy where honor killings (protecting the *honor* of the family) are the norm: "You touch it [a piece of food being offered by a woman], her nearest male relative will have to try to kill you." When the top tribal leader is killed, his young wife (who is pregnant) is duty bound to kill herself. Like Saudi Arabia, Capella Four is of great strategic importance because of its mineral wealth: "The rare mineral topaline, vital to the life-support systems of planetoid colonies, has been discovered in abundance here." Additionally, "Mudd's Women" (1966) highlights the historic practice of sending women to the frontier for purposes of matching them with a husband.[14] Harvey Mudd traffics women to wealthy men that mine precious minerals on barren, forbidding planets. Episode "Bread and Circuses" (1968) — Captain Kirk is offered a slave for sexual pleasure.

"Turnabout Intruder" is distinct in American popular culture for its glaring critique of the discrimination that women faced at the time. The prejudices that women face on a regular basis have driven Janice Lester insane. It is observed that "Janice has driven herself mad with jealousy, hatred and ambition"—ostensibly because society placed artificial, arbitrary (maddening) limits upon her.

While on "Camus Two... exploring the ruins of a dead civilization", Lester had almost her entire scientific team murdered and is feigning illness. She has manufactured a crisis to lure Captain Kirk into a trap. Lester has discovered an ancient device that allows her to switch her consciousness with that of Captain Kirk—a former lover. Kirk says he had to break off the romantic relationship with Lester because she holds "intense hatred of her own womanhood." Lester is "alone" (unmarried) because of her ambitions, but they are unfulfilled precisely because she is a woman. Upon executing her plan and taking over Kirk's body, she declares to him (in Lester's body): "Now you

---

14 Albert L. Hurtado, *Intimate Frontiers: Sex, Gender, and Culture in Old California* (Albuquerque: University of New Mexico Press, 1999).

know the indignity of being a woman... it's better to be dead than to live alone in the body of a woman. It's better to be dead."

Lester says of Kirk: "I love the life he led. The *power* of a starship commander." Lester denounces the discrimination (unfairness) that women experienced at the time: "Your world of starship captains doesn't admit women. It isn't fair." Lead character, Mary Richards, of the *Mary Tyler Moore Show* was promoted from "Associate Producer" to "Producer" of the evening news for a local television station. The character, however, was not ambitious nor confrontational about (un)equal opportunities in the workplace.[15]

Anti-Racism

The television series *Star Trek* was a salient victory for the U.S. civil rights movement of the 1960s[16], and arguably played a key role in ending the open, official proclamation of white supremacy in the American South.[17] The series aired when the civil rights movement was being attacked as part of a global communist conspiracy and the practice of lynching was still alive.[18]

Somewhat surprisingly, however, *Star Trek* (the original series) is cast as unfair to ethnic minorities—including African Americans. André M. Carrington, in *Speculative Blackness: The Future of Race in Science Fiction*, stands out on this score.[19] Carrington takes an ahistorical tack and denounces the fact that the character of Lt. Uhura (the one African-American bridge

---

15 Kutulas, *After Aquarius Dawned*, 95–96.
16 Bruce J. Dierenfield, *The Civil Rights Movement*, rev. ed. (New York: Routledge, 2014); George A. Gonzalez, "'May we Together Become Greater' ": in Defence of Star Trek and Anti-Racism," *Foundation: The International Review of Science Fiction* 50, no. 138 (2021): 14–22.
17 Drew Gilpin Faust, *The Creation of Confederate Nationalism: Ideology and Identity in the Civil War South* (Baton Rouge: Louisiana State University Press, 1988); Adam H. Domby, *The False Cause: Fraud, Fabrication, and White Supremacy in Confederate Memory* (Charlottesville: University of Virginia Press, 2020); Robert D. McFadden, "John M. Patterson, 99, Governor Who Backed Klan in Alabama, Dies," *New York Times*, June 7, 2021, A22.
18 M. J. Heale, *McCarthy's Americans: Red Scare Politics in State and Nation, 1935–1965* (Athens: University of Georgia Press, 1998); Jeff Woods, *Black Struggle, Red Scare: Segregation and Anti-Communism in the South, 1948–1968* (Baton Rouge: Louisiana State University, 2004).
19 André M. Carrington, *Speculative Blackness: The Future of Race in Science Fiction* (Minneapolis: University of Minnesota Press, 2016).

officer in the original series) was a supporting role. The significance of Uhura to the civil rights movement of the era is indicated by the fact that according to Nichelle Nichols (who played Uhura) when she was thinking of leaving the series no less than Martin Luther King, Jr. asked her to continue on the show.[20] It is also noteworthy that in "The Ultimate Computer" (1968) an African American plays one of leading minds of the Federation, and in the episode "Court Martial" an American African is cast as an admiral. All are a direct rejection (mocking) of the white supremacy that was prevalent in the U.S. South at the time—as indicated by the fact that the rabidly racist/ segregationist George Wallace won five Deep South states in the presidential election of 1968.[21]

An affirmative nod to the civil rights movement is found in the Star Trek portrayal of Abraham Lincoln—the "Great Emancipator".[22] As noted in Chapter 3, in *Star Trek* Lincoln is cast as a figure that forwarded progressive modernism— on a worldwide basis.[23] With the characters of Uhura and Lincoln, the creators of Star Trek are directly, unambiguously defying/challenging the Jim Crow South. The episode "Let that Be Your Last Battlefield" is an explicit and pointed critique, rejection of Southern race hatred.

An Anti-Jim Crow Polemic

Perhaps what is most glaring in Carrington's critique of the identity (*race*) politics of the Star Trek franchise is the fact that he does not make any comment on the original series episode "Let That Be Your Last Battlefield"—an episode

---

20 Nichelle Nichols, *Beyond Uhura – Star Trek and Other Memories* (New York: G. P. Putnam's Sons, 1994), 164–165.
21 Dan T. Carter, *The Politics of Rage: George Wallace, the Origins of the New Conservatism, and the Transformation of American Politics*, 2nd ed. (Baton Rouge: Louisiana State University, 2000).
22 James M. McPherson, *Abraham Lincoln and the Second American Revolution* (New York: Oxford University Press, 1992); James Oakes, *Freedom National: The Destruction of Slavery in the United States* (New York: W.W. Norton & Company, 2012); Gregory P. Downs, *The Second American Revolution: The Civil War-Era Struggle over Cuba and the Rebirth of the American Republic* (Chapel Hill: University of North Caroline Press, 2019).
23 Modernism is a set of normative values that privileges reason and secularism, as opposed to obscurantism and political religion (i.e., theocracy). Peter Childs, *Modernism*, 3rd ed. (New York: Routledge, 2016).

that is explicitly anti-racist.[24] The Enterprise crew comes into contact with an alien race that is half white and half black, but part of the population is white on the right side and the other is white on the left side. The Enterprise crew cannot fathom that such a trivial difference would be politically, socially significant for anyone—much less fuel the intense hatred and violence that the two alien individuals on-board the Enterprise (Lokai and Bele) direct toward one another (each one from the different ethnic groups).

Most significantly, the alien characters replicate the debate surrounding the 1960s civil rights movement—including *race supremacy*. The member of the oppressed caste reprises the history of Southern slavery—Lokai: they "tore us from our families, herded us together like cattle and then sold us as slaves!" The representative of the dominate group conveys the condescension, paternalism of the Southern Lost Cause false narrative—Bele: "They were savages... We took them into our hearts, our homes." Bele continues: "Slaves?... You were freed." Ostensibly referring to the conditions of the Jim Crow South, Lokai: "Freed? Were we free to be men? Free to be husbands and fathers? Free to live our lives in equality and dignity?" Overtly defending race based casteism—Bele: "There is an order in things [...] It is obvious to the most simpleminded that Lokai is of an inferior breed." Lokai, later speaking to the Enterprise crew, asks them (really, the audience) to empathize with the profound injustice and wanton violence that people of his ethnicity (really, African Americans) endure:

> How can you understand my fear, my apprehension, my degradation, my suffering?... How can I make your flesh know how it feels to see all those who are like you, and only because they are like you, despised, slaughtered, and even worse, denied the simplest bit of decency that is a living being's right?

In the end we learn that the racism of this civilization resulted in its destruction.

It is significant that in the denouement of the episode Uhura proclaims that the behavior of these aliens "doesn't make any sense." She resides in a world of ethnic equality and fairness and cannot understand how people could hate so profoundly over something like skin tone. Spock, a Vulcan who works among humans, is similarly incredulous: "To expect sense from two mentalities of such extreme viewpoints is not logical." The point is made by the Enterprise crew that "There was persecution on Earth once [...] but it happened way back in the

---

24 Bernardi (*Star Trek and History*) is someone else who critiques *Star Trek* for its treatment of race/ethnicity and overlooks the anti-racist episode "Let That Be Your Last Battlefield".

twentieth century. There's no such primitive thinking today." The future is ethnic equality and a rejection of race casteism as *primitive thinking*.

The original series episode "Cloud Minders" (as outlined in Chapter 1) depicts a society (the planet of Ardana) where torture technology ("the rays") and racism are used to maintain/stabilize a caste system. The leader of Adrana, in justifying the use of torture, spews overt racism: Troglytes are "a conglomerate of inferior species." Enterprise's Doctor McCoy, in referring to Adrana's leader and the fact that race hatred is politically, intellectually (morally) blinding, dryly notes, "It's pretty hard to overcome prejudice."

Racism was deployed to unite the American public in fighting the Cold War.[25] In the original series episode "Day of the Dove" an alien is surreptitiously impelling animosity between the Enterprise crew and Klingons on board—including promoting "race hatred".

Conclusion

Star Trek (original series) is a historically important feminist and anti-racist (justice) text. Star Trek of the 1960s was a major blow to the Jim Crow U.S. South—arguably the nail in its coffin. Millions of Americans viewed a future totally free of ethnic biases—where African Americans (along with everyone else) are able to reach the highest echelons of society. While Star Trek was without question a metaphor for ethnic/gender justice and fairness, the original series also directly, unambiguously challenged the Jim Crow South—"Let that Be Your Last Battlefield". Additionally, the original series took on the proponents of anti-communism—many of which who sought to stigmatize and repress the civil right movement by denouncing it as part of a global communist cabal.

Star Trek of the 1960s has not received its due as a significant factor in the defeat of Jim Crow. There is little question that the original series exposed the lie and stupidity of ethnic bigotry. With such characters as Lt. Uhura, Abraham Lincoln, and Lokai, Star Trek played a glaring role in making the claims of the civil rights movement commonsensical—whereas (Southern) white supremacy and racial hatred were treated as fundamentally backward, as well as inherently malevolent and destructive

Importantly, Star Trek openly identified the oppressive and destructive aspects of 1950s patriarchy. The pigeonholing of women into marriage; a disfiguring etiquette; the forcing of women to choose between marriage or career; as

25   Woods, *Black Struggle, Red Scare*.

well as the debilitating discrimination against women who sought careers. *Star Trek* also portrayed the historic (ongoing) mistreatment of women—as currency; sex slaves; their killing to maintain family honor. *Star Trek* featured strong, capable female characters. Characters that defiantly challenged patriarchy and were sharply politically cognizant.

· 5 ·
STAR TREK AND THE PROGRESSIVE DIALECTIC: THE DEPICTION OF THE MARXIST ONTOLOGY OF JUSTICE

As noted in chapter one, Karl Marx initially identified the *progressive dialectic*, and Leon Trotsky—as leader of the Russian Revolution—acted upon it. The "United Federation of Planets"—the fictional interstellar political entity in Star Trek which humans lead—is the artistic representation of the progressive dialectic. The failure to pursue the *progressive dialectic* is to precipitate disaster for humanity. Star Trek (in conveying the progressive dialectic) makes the specific argument that if humanity/civilization is to survive/thrive the achieving of a modern classless society, totally free of ethnic, gender biases (*justice*) must be a priority. This requires that capitalist values be abandoned and neoliberalism has to be replaced.

Star Trek and Capitalism

Star Trek explicitly rejects capitalism in *The Next Generation* episode "The Neutral Zone" (1988): in the 24th century "People are no longer obsessed with the accumulation of 'things'. We have eliminated hunger, want, the need for possessions." The purpose of life is to "To improve yourself... enrich yourself."

Star Trek: Discovery (2017 to 2024): "capitalism" is expressly linked to slavery[1] and predatory foreign policy machinations ("There Is a Tide..." 2021).

In the *Deep Space Nine* episode "In the Cards" (1997) it is explained that humanity "abandoned currency-based economics in favor of [a] philosophy of self-enhancement." *Star Trek: Lower Decks* (2020–) (set in the 24th century) mocks the concept of currency—happening upon a holographic bank: "I think this is what people used to use to store their money [...] Uh, yes, hello... I'd like to withdraw some paper with no intrinsic value" ("Room For Growth" 2022). The notion of a society being governed by a "philosophy of self-enhancement" mirrors Karl Marx's point that in moving from capitalism to communism society would go "From each according to his ability, to each according to his needs!"—i.e., communist politics would focus on "the all-around development of the individual."[2] Also noted in the episode "In the Cards", in the world of Star Trek people "work to better [themselves] and the rest of Humanity."

The episode "Little Green Men" (1995—*Deep Space Nine*) indicates that humans (Americans) of the 20th century (shaped by capitalist values) are "crude, gullible and greedy." Marx offers a similar rebuke of the cultural/social ethos of capitalists: "Contempt for theory, art, history, and for man as an end in himself... is the real, conscious standpoint, the virtue of the man of money."[3] The observation is made in the episode that humans of the 20th century are "not like the ones from the [24th century] Federation." Star Trek is optimistic insofar as (without capitalism distorting society's values) humans will collectively achieve a higher plane of intelligence; knowledge; and emotional maturity. This is the promise of the progressive dialectic and the Enlightenment. (An optimism shared by Marx: in "communist society... the all-round development of the individual" will be achieved.[4]

---

1 Siddharth Kara, *Modern Slavery: A Global Perspective* (New York: Columbia University Press, 2017).
2 Karl Marx, *The Critique of the Gotha Programme* (London: Electric Book Co., 2001 [1875]), 20.
3 Karl Marx, *On the Jewish Question*, 1844, http://www.marxists.org/archive/marx/works/1844/jewish-question/.
4 Marx, *The Critique of the Gotha Programme*, 20

Neoliberalism

Drawing from the Star Trek text, the *progressive dialectic* begins with the American Revolutionary War (see below), followed by the U.S. Civil War (see below). Star Trek fictionally completes America's *revolutionary circle* with the Bell Uprising. Aired in 1995, "Past Tense" (*Deep Space Nine*) is centered on this fictional uprising. The characters Sisko, Bashir, and Dax are accidentally sent back to 2024 San Francisco. They encounter the San Francisco "Sanctuary District"—an urban zone where untold numbers of the poor and dispossessed are forcibly interned: "by the early twenty-twenties there was a place like this in every major city in the United States"—dirty, dilapidated, and overcrowded with "people without jobs or places to live." Sanctuary Districts are a metaphor for the de-industrialization, job loss, and disinvestment that major American urban areas (such as Detroit[5] and Cleveland[6]) experienced as a result of neoliberal global capitalism[7]—with much of U.S. industry moving to cheaper labor venues.[8] Additionally, "Past Tense" makes reference to the process of technology replacing or displacing employment.[9] A Sanctuary District resident explains that "they laid a bunch of us off when they got some new equipment... and so I ended up here."

The vital need for civilization to institute humane politics/values is made clear in "Past Tense". Sisko inadvertently obstructs the Bell Uprising. Like the victory of the Nazis in World War Two ("City on the Edge of Forever"

---

5   Thomas J. Sugrue, *The Origins of the Urban Crisis: Race and Inequality in Postwar Detroit* (Princeton: Princeton University Press, 2005); Joe Drape, "Bankruptcy for Ailing Detroit, but Prosperity for Its Teams," *New York Times*, Oct. 14., 2013, A1; Mitch Smith, "10 Years After Filing for Bankruptcy, Detroit Has a Long To-Do List," *New York Times*, July 16, 2023, A12.
6   Carol Poh Miller and Robert Wheeler, *Cleveland: A Concise History* (Bloomington: Indiana University Press, 2009).
7   Guin A. McKee, *The Problem of Jobs: Liberalism, Race, and Deindustrialization in Philadelphia* (Chicago: University of Chicago Press, 2009); Timothy Williams, "For Shrinking Cities, Destruction Is a Path to Renewal," *New York Times*, Nov. 12, 2013, A15.
8   Mary Elizabeth Gallagher, *Contagious Capitalism: Globalization and the Politics of Labor in China* (Princeton: Princeton University Press, 2005); Kelly Sims Gallagher, *China Shifts Gears: Automakers, Oil, Pollution, and Development* (Cambridge, MA: MIT Press, 2006).
9   James Steinhoff, *Automation and Autonomy: Labour, Capital and Machines in the Artificial Intelligence Industry* (New York: Palgrave Macmillan, 2021); Steve Lohr, "A.I. Threatens Lawyers? We've Heard This Before," *New York Times*, Apr. 10, 2023, B1; Ben Ryder Howe, "Scouting Out The Next Wave Of Robot Workers," *New York Times*, July 30, 2023, BU6.

1967—*Star Trek*), this erases the entire history of the Federation. Meanwhile, back in the 24th century, all that remains of the original time line is the ship (the Defiant) that beamed Sisko, Bashir, and Dax to the past. Uncertain when Sisko *et al.* are located, members of the Defiant crew randomly transport into Earth's past. They conclude Sisko *et al.* were sent to some period prior to 2048: "that wasn't the mid-twenty-first century that I read about in school. It's been changed. *Earth history had its rough patches, but never that rough.*" Therefore, the absence of the Bell Uprising to start the revolution that would politically challenge the current neoliberalism regime would seemingly result in Earth's society transforming into some type of dysfunctional (chaotic) scenario as early as 2048. To take the argument further, the inability of humanity to move away from the current neoliberalism capitalist regime would result in the *end of history*. This is parallel with Rosa Luxemburg's prediction that the "future is either socialism or barbarism."[10]

Consonant with an interpretation of Star Trek as depicting American history as a series of progressive *revolutionary* events are the original series episodes "The Savage Curtain" and "The Omega Glory". In the episode "The Omega Glory" Kirk explains to a primitive people that worship the U.S. Constitution that this document "was not written for chiefs or kings or warriors or the rich and powerful, but for all the people!" Kirk therefore invokes the revolutionary significance of *equality before the law*—"All Men are Created Equal" (the American Revolution and the Constitution that followed). He declares that rights and freedom "must apply to everyone or they mean nothing!" In "The Savage Curtain" the Enterprise crew meets the incarnation of Abraham Lincoln. Kirk insists that the crew treat him with the respect and deference due this great historical figure—the leader of the second American Revolution (the U.S. Civil War and the resulting elimination of chattel slavery).[11]

My argument is that within the Star Trek text the *progressive dialectic* is depicted: the American Revolution; the U.S. Civil War; the Fight Against Fascism ("City on the End of Forever"); the Bell Uprising (i.e., the defeat of neoliberalism). These are necessary stops on the road to (global) utopia—a

10 Paul Frölich, *Rosa Luxemburg: Her Life and Work* (New York: Howard Fertig, 1969); Stephen Eric Bronner, *Rosa Luxemburg: A Revolutionary for Our Times* (University Park: Pennsylvania State University Press, 1993).
11 James M. McPherson, *Abraham Lincoln and the Second American Revolution* (New York: Oxford University Press, 1992); James Oakes, *Freedom National: The Destruction of Slavery in the United States* (New York: W.W. Norton & Company, 2012).

modern classless society, free of gender, ethnic biases. American Marxists have historically held that the United States is engaged in an unfolding revolutionary process. Trotskyists (followers of Leon Trotsky)—operating in the U.S. since the 1920s—hold that the American Revolution and the Civil War will be completed by the socialist revolution (the Bell Uprising[?]) and the creation of the workers' state.[12] (It is noteworthy and significant that in the episode where the Bell Uprising is conveyed the phrase "Neo-Trotskists" is used; also, in another episode, a passage from the Communist Manifesto is read.[13])

Conclusion

From the Hegel, Marx philosophical canon two distinct, yet related theories of beauty can be deduced. First, there is the spirit of beauty—whereby what humans' consider beautiful is derived from the universal Hegelian *spirit of beauty*. Significantly, the *spirit of justice* has a very important role in determining what is beautiful. The *spirit of justice* informing the beautiful is especially significant in the realm of popular culture. Hegel and Marx do differ on the evolution, elevation of humanity. For Hegel, society becomes more just, fair as a result of the interaction of ideas over time (*idealism*). Marx, in contradistinction, points to the interaction of *social classes* and the *means of the production* as a prime driver of social evolution/progress. The Star Trek text is very popular and philosophically significant because it portrays justice as a modern, classless society (totally free of ethnic, gender biases). Additionally, humanity's history in the Star Trek franchise is marked by progressive revolutionary moments/events—hence, the Marxist *progressive dialectic*. For this reason (I submit) the franchise is beautiful (entertaining) and draws a massive, enduring audience.

---

12 Bryan D. Palmer, *James P. Cannon and the Origins of the American Revolutionary Left, 1890–1928* (Urbana: University of Illinois Press, 2010), and *James P. Cannon and the Emergence of Trotskyism in the United States, 1928-38* (Boston: Brill, 2022); Paul Le Blanc, Alan Wald, and George Breitman, eds., *Trotskyism in the United States: Historical Essays and Reconsiderations*, 2nd ed. (Chicago: Haymarket Books, 2016).

13 In the midst of a labor strike (*Deep Space Nine*—"Bar Association" 1996), a character reads directly from the *Communist Manifesto*: "Workers of the world, unite. You have nothing to lose but your chains."

· 6 ·

THE BOYS AND *JUSTICE LEAGUE UNLIMITED*: THE SUPER HERO AS METAPHORICAL OF GLOBAL (IN)JUSTICE

While American comic book superheroes may tilt toward the nation and even U.S. foreign policy,[1] the television animated series, *Justice League Unlimited*, stands out for its globalism, and, specifically, its treatment of neoliberalism (authoritarianism and wealth inequality). Particularly noteworthy is the critique of American militarism offered in the show. *Justice League* (2001–2004) draws on the DC Comics stable of superhero characters: Superman; Wonder Woman; The Flash; Martian Manhunter (a.k.a. J'onn J'onzz, pronounced Jon Jones); Batman; Hawk Girl; and the Green Lantern. The show is later retitled *Justice League Unlimited* (2004–2006) and groups together innumerable superheroes.[2]

Jason Dittmer, in *Captain America and the Nationalist Superhero*, holds that "superheroes are co-constitutive elements of both American identity and the U.S. government's foreign policy practices." He adds that "the nationalist superhero... speaks most clearly to a phenomenon that has been at the center of work in the field of critical geopolitics: the state-centrism that has become

---

1 William J. Savage, *Comic Books and America, 1945–1954* (Norman: University of Oklahoma Press, 1990).
2 George A. Gonzalez, "*Justice League Unlimited* and the Politics of Globalization," *Foundation: The International Review of Science Fiction* 45, no. 123 (2016): 5-13.

the focus of political thought over the past century."³ The Amazon Prime television series *The Boys* (2019 to present) critiques the nationalist superhero by presenting him as a metaphor for the pathologies of American corporate capitalism. Writing in his 1945 essay "The Comics and the Super State," Walter Ong rendered a sharp critique of what he identified as the dangerous nationalism within the superhero genre:

> There are titles like *Captain America* that tie up the destinies of our country with those of a hero.... The comics's habit of tinkering with the notion of the hero as the emotional correlative of the whole nation marches exactly the technique of Hitler, who was the prototype and hero of those who wanted to be "typical Germans".⁴

The creators of *The Boys* satirize, critique the superhero genre and its historic promotion of U.S. nationalism along the lines posited by Ong. The lead superhero in the series is Homelander (whose cape is an American flag). He is a hero only in terms of corporate propaganda, as in fact Homelander is a murderous sociopath—who uses American nationalism and conservative religion⁵ as a cover.

In sharp contrast to the Nationalist Superhero outlined by Omg, Dittmer, and *The Boys*, the Justice League television series of the 2000s makes a case for global justice, government. Moreover, *Justice League*, in a way that no other American television series does, treats the fact that the U.S. is seeking to maintain its hegemony in a neoliberal world through rampant and ominous militarism. *The Boys* casts the U.S. "war on terror" and even crime fighting as cynical public relations means to convert the state into a modern day corporate-controlled leviathan. For its part, *The Boys* (after years of brutal war in countries as Iraq and Afghanistan) is unflinching in conveying gore (typical of such conflicts)—with heads exploding as well as being crushed.

---

3 Jason Dittmer, *Captain America and the Nationalist Superhero* (Philadelphia: Temple University Press, 2012), 2–3.
4 Walter Ong, "The Comics and the Super State." In *The Superhero Reader*, Charles Hatfield, Jeet Heer, and Kent Worcester, eds. (Jackson: University Press of Mississippi, 2013), 37-38.
5 Homelander and his superhero cohort openly associate with the Christian group "Samaritan's Embrace"—which advocates a conservative social, political agenda.

Modernity and the Superhero

The super hero genre was first established in the late 1930s once technologies/sciences like aviation; communication; armament (e.g., tanks); chemistry, etc. were well established/popularized. Superman, the first major comic book superhero (1938), has a moniker that overtly invokes industry ("Man of Steel"). Perhaps no superhero is more a function/product of modernity than Batman, who has no superpowers other than being a great scientist/chemist/engineer. Moreover, as a capitalist with seemingly unlimited wealth, Batman (who as Bruce Wayne controls Wayne Industries) can directly employ factories (industrial infrastructure) to produce his super-gadgets/instruments.

The creation of the super hero genre also coincides with the rise of fascism. As the political situation deteriorated both in Europe and the Pacific, Americans could readily envision the powers of modernity (i.e., super heroes) protecting them from these threats. When the U.S. enters World War Two it deploys its industrial might to fight. One way to imagine/conceive of this war machine is through the personage of Captain America—who is the result of advanced chemistry (a "serum").[6]

In *The Boys*'s super heroes (referred to as "Supes") are also the result of a serum—which is injected into infants (itself a sinister turn). Superheroes are created in this instance not to fight for justice, protection of the innocent, but for corporate profits. With *The Boys*, unlike Batman, super heroes are not only of corporations, but they are for corporations. Put differently, Batman is a product of corporate wealth and power, whereas *The Boys*'s super heroes serve corporate America—the multi-billion dollar Vought corporation.

The creators of *The Boys* identify public relations (in conjunction with a compliant corporate media[7]) as a superpower—creating the myth of selfless, humane "superheroes" and vilifying "super villains". The "heroes" of Vought generate massive income through movies, television shows, and payments from various local governments in exchange for crime fighting. These movies, shows and the publicizing of the crime fighting in turn serve to politically aggrandize/lionize Vought and its super heroes. In fact, Vought's heroes use wanton death, destruction to serve their own agendas—including

---

6 Dittmer, *Captain America and the Nationalist Superhero*, 93–97.
7 Victor Pickard, *Democracy without Journalism?: Confronting the Misinformation Society* (New York: Oxford University Press, 2020).

incorporation into the U.S. military (where the heroes report directly to the Vought corporate leadership) ("Nothing Like It in the World" 2020).

A particularly cynical maneuver is that Vought created the very super villains its propaganda uses to protect and expand its political power. Similarly, the American government has armed the same Islamic religious militant groups that it publicly rails against[8] and uses to justify its military adventurism as well as its drone assassination program.[9]

Through the *Deep Space Nine* platform, Star Trek's creators issue a clear warning that political elites can/do use stability (safety/security) concerns to establish regimes of dictatorship. In the denouement of "Homefront" (1996) Earth experiences a planetary-wide blackout. A state of emergency has been declared. We learn that the power outage was perpetrated by elements within Starfleet (the Federation's military apparatus) in an effort to justify a military dictatorship ("Paradise Lost" 1996). Thus, *Deep Space Nine* issues a caution against the use of national security threats to suspend civil and political rights, as well as democratic decision-making processes.

During season two of *The Boys*, the Vought hero Stormfront uses her fame to foment xenophobic elements—using the specter of dangerous super villains seeking to enter the country. Through right-wing rabble rousing, Stormfront claims she has an "army of 5000" shock troops ("We Gotta Go Now" 2020). In the contemporary period former President Trump uses his stature and visibility to encourage violent right-wing groups.[10] During the 2020 election Trump consistently *ramped up* his supporters through the regularly repeated fantasy that there was a conspiracy to steal the election from him—resulting in the storming of the U.S. Capitol Building on Jan. 6th, 2021.[11] More broadly,

---

8   David E. Sanger, "Rebel Arms Flow Is Said to Benefit Jihadists in Syria," *New York Times*, Oct. 15, 2012, A1.
9   Eric Schmitt, Thomas Gibbons-Neff, Charlie Savage and Helene Cooper, "Trump Is Said to Plan Reduction of Forces in Afghanistan, Iraq and Somalia," *New York Times*, Nov. 17, 2020, A13.
10 Nicholas Kristof, "Trump Calls On Extremists To 'Stand By'," *New York Times*, Oct. 1, 2020, A27; Alan Feuer, "Testimony of Trump Allies And Extremists at Hearing," *New York Times*, June 30, 2022, A17; Linda Qiu, "How Bragg And Soros Are Linked," *New York Times*, Mar. 24, 2023, A16; Jonathan Weisman, and Andrew Higgins, "Behind Indictment, Right Wing Sees a Familiar Villain in Soros," *New York Times*, Apr. 5, 2023, A17; Maggie Haberman, and Jonathan Swan, "Trump Had Wanted Activist Who Targets Muslims," *New York Times*, Apr. 8, 2023, A15..
11 Adam Goldman, and Shaila Dewan, "Shouting, Smashed Glass, A Lunge, Then a Gunshot," *New York Times*, Jan. 24, 2021, A1; Alan Feuer, "A Few Main Characters Form the Core of the Committee's Narrative," *New York Times*, June 10, 2022, A16.

Trump has assailed science and civility, even rationality[12]—including his continued insistence that the 2020 election was stolen.[13]

The audience ultimately learns that Stormfront was a contemporary of Hitler and intimately acquainted with the Nazi leadership. She continues to hold virulently racist views ("The Bloody Doors Off" 2020). The character Stormfront can be read as a metaphorical suggestion that there is a line between the Nazis of the 1930s and 1940s and the Trump-led American government. President Trump himself invoked a central aspect of Nazism when he declaimed *"that America will never be a socialist country"*[14]—thereby manifesting a hate of socialism/communism/Bolshevism.[15] Additionally, President Trump openly promoted (twittered) "white power"[16]– the ideological core of Nazism.[17]

Whereas the Vought super heroes represent nationalism, xenophobia, obscurant religion, the Justice League reflects the current/highest stage of modernity—globalization. In terms of symbolism, super heroes readily traveling all over the world and into space conveys the reality of our globalized world. Indicative of a globalist outlook, the league in *Justice League* (*Unlimited*) has its headquarters in a space station (the "Watchtower") orbiting the planet—outside the Earth's nation-state system. The Watchtower (i.e., space) as the base of operation for the Justice League is particularly significant because

---

12 Alexander Burns, Jonathan Martin, and Maggie Haberman, "Trump Escalates Push to Erode Trust in Vote," *New York Times*, Oct. 1, 2020, A1; Christopher Flavelle, and Lisa Friedman, "President Acts To Undermine Science Agency," *New York Times*, Oct. 28, 2020, A1.
13 Luke Broadwater, and Maggie Haberman, "Trump Reply To Congress Repeats Lies On Election," *New York Times*, Oct. 15, 2022, A17.
14 As quoted in Anita Kumar, "Decoding Trump's speech before the United Nations," *Politico*, Sept. 24, 2019. Web.
15 Volker Ullrich, *Hitler: Ascent, 1889-1939* (New York: Knof, 2016).
16 Michael D. Shear, "Trump Amplifies 'White Power' on Twitter" *New York Times*, June 29, 2020, A15.
17 Kathleen Belew, *Bring the War Home: The White Power Movement and Paramilitary America* (Cambridge, MA: Harvard University Press, 2018), and "Militant Whiteness in the Age of Trump," in *The Presidency of Donald J. Trump: A First Historical Assessment*, ed. Julian E. Zelizer (Princeton: Princeton University Press, 2022); Michael H. Keller, and David D. Kirkpatrick, "Suspicion and Blame as Their America Vanishes," *New York Times*, Oct. 24, 2022, A1; Charles M. Blow, "Whitewashing White Nationalism," *New York Times*, July 16, 2023, SR3.

historically virtually all American comic book heroes operate from the U.S., and especially New York City.[18]

The Vought superheroes operate out of New York. In the first episode of season two, Homelander is overseeing a focus group testing different public relations ideas. When the group expresses a clear preference for the slogan "Saving the World" over "Saving America", Homelander vehemently rejects the group's opinion and opts for the latter slogan ("The Big Ride" 2020).

Whereas the Vought "Seven" (the prime group of *supes*) promotes nationalism and the nation-state system, the Justice League operates outside of government jurisdiction. The league maintains a space-based weapon (a "fusion cannon") in the face of objections from the U.S. President: "I've repeatedly expressed my strongest disapproval of you guys having that space cannon floating over everyone's heads" ("Flashpoint" 2005). As noted above, Vought machinations result in its super heroes being incorporated into the American military ("Nothing Like It in the World").

Reflective of the global outlook of the Justice League in the 2000s, one 2005 episode has Wonder Woman confronting world leaders for insufficient action on climate change. Casting climate change as a security concern, Wonder Woman warns world leaders "you have to take this seriously" and threatens a "military solution" ("To Another Shore").

Democracy

While the *Justice League (Unlimited)* television series, contrary to the norm of the superhero genre, communicates globalism—as opposed to nationalism, it also conveys the inherent lack of democracy in the operation of the current world system. The superhero genre *in toto* seemingly suggests that democracy within the context of present-day modernity is an impossibility.[19] In the context of capitalism the powers of modernity are directed by capitalists—who pursue wealth, power, ego gratification, etc. Significantly, there is no election, or democratic process, to determine who will gain super powers, and, similarly, there is no mechanism that would allow the public to take away such powers.[20]

---

18 Richard Reynolds, *Super Heroes: A Modern Mythology* (Jackson: University Press of Mississippi, 1992), 19.
19 Ibid., 15.
20 Terry Kading, "Drawn into 9/11, But Where Have all the Superheroes Gone?," in Jeff McLaughlin, ed. *Comics as Philosophy* (Jackson: University of Mississippi, 2005).

The Boys is explicitly centered on the idea that elites are above the law and democratic control. The "Supes" engage in murder and mayhem with absolute impunity. The series begins when a Supe (named A-Train) literally runs through a woman on the street—splaying her open. Vought public relations (passively accepted by the media) is that A-Train was responding to a bank robbery and the woman was in the middle of the street—both demonstrably false ("The Name of the Game" 2019). Season two ends with Homelander floating above New York while masturbating—yelling "I CAN DO WHATEVER I WANT" ("What I Know" 2020).

Significantly, Vought seeks to cover-up A-Train's killing of the woman (while he was on drugs) by handing out money (settlements) and having Non-Disclosure Agreements (NDAs) signed by those receiving payments. "Settlements" and NDAs can be interpreted as a Billionaire superpower. This was brought to light during the 2020 debates among hopefuls for the Democratic Party presidential nomination. Billionaire presidential candidate Michael Bloomberg has a history of making ugly sexist comments in mixed company as well as engaging in sexual harassment. Complainants were silenced with pay-offs and NDAs.[21] Daniel Snyder, the billionaire owner of the Washington Commanders (an American football team), also used pay-offs and NDAs to cover-up allegations of over two decades of serial sexual misconduct.[22] Mere mortals' careers, even lives, would be destroyed by such serial abuse.

The George W. Bush White House declared itself above the law with the theory of the Unitary Executive, whereby the White House controls the executive branch; Congress as well as the courts (i.e., the law) are purely advisory.[23] The Bush government wantonly invaded Iraq on the pretext of lies (see

---

21 Maggie Astor, "Elizabeth Warren, Criticizing Bloomberg, Sent a Message: She Won't Be Ignored," *New York Times*, Feb. 19, 2020. Web.

22 Committee on Oversight and Reform (U.S. House of Representatives), *Conduct Detrimental: How the NFL and the Washington Commanders Covered Up Decades of Sexual Misconduct* (Washington, DC: Government Printing Office, Dec. 8, 2022); Ken Belson, and Katherine Rosman, "Congress Slams N.F.L. and the Owner of the Washington Commanders," *New York Times*, Dec. 9, 2022, B7; Ken Belson, and Katherine Rosman, "Snyder Agrees to Sell Commanders for $6 Billion," *New York Times*, April 14, 2023, B6; Ken Belson, and Jenny Vrentas, "After Investigation, Snyder Faces $60 Million Fine," *New York Times*, July 21, 2023, B8.

23 Ryan J. Barilleaux, and Christopher S. Kelley, eds., *The Unitary Executive and the Modern Presidency* (College Station: Texas A&M University Press, 2010); Charlie Savage, and Maggie Haberman, "An Advocate of Presidential Power Interests Trump for Attorney General," *New York Times*, Dec. 7, 2018, A15; Peter Baker, "Trump's Insults End a Brief

above). It instituted policies of torture ("enhanced interrogation"), indefinite detention without trial ("enemy combatants"), and kidnaping ("extraordinary rendition").[24] The Obama administration (2009–2017) expanded and institutionalized drone assassination—where people are killed without trial or a modicum of due process.[25] The American president, Donald J. Trump, openly acted like a dictator—declaring falsely that the U.S. Constitution gave him as President "the right to do whatever I want."[26] He defied congressional subpoenas;[27] and congressional budgetary decisions;[28] as well as publicly refused to abide by Supreme Court rulings.[29]

Somewhat presaging the George Floyd killing protests of 2020, it is solely the public that tries to hold the Vought Supes accountable. A protest ensues after footage is made public showing Homelander killing a bystander during an anti-terrorist operation ("We Gotta Go Now").

With *Justice League Unlimited* we see the league overtly taking on the role of a government—identifying risks/crises throughout the world (even the galaxy) and deploying the appropriate response (i.e., superheroes). One scene conveys the league overseeing/conducting "23 active missions" ("To Another Shore"). The Justice League, for instance, evacuates people threatened by

---

Civil Interlude," *New York Times*, Dec. 8, 2018, A10; Emily Cochrane, "A Passive Congress Enables Trump to Use Pulpit to Continue His Shutdown Chatter," *New York Times*, Dec. 25, 2018, A15; Charles Blow M., "An Imperial Presidency?" *New York Times*, May 13, 2019, A19; Katie Benner, "Legal Opinions Support Executive Privilege," *New York Times*, Dec. 13, 2019, A17; Jonathan Swan, Charlie Savage, and Maggie Haberman, "Trump and Allies Seeking Vast Increase of His Power," *New York Times*, July 17, 2023, A1.

24 Terry H. Anderson, *Bush's Wars* (New York: Oxford University Press, 2011); Carol Rosenberg, "U.N. Rebukes U.S. Torture Of Saudi Man At Cuba Base," *New York Times*, June 5, 2023, A10, and "Judge to Decide Whether C.I.A. Torture's Taint Stretched to Guantánamo," *New York Times*, July 1, 2023, A20.

25 Charlie Savage, "Order Limits Report of Deaths From U.S. Airstrikes," *New York Times*, Mar. 7, 2019, A14.

26 As quoted in Michael Brice-Saddler, "While bemoaning Mueller Probe, Trump Falsely Says the Constitution Gives Him 'the right to do whatever I want'," *Washington Post*, July 23, 2019. Web.

27 Adam Liptak, "This Clash Might Have Made the Framers Gasp," *New York Times*, May 8, 2019, A1.

28 Peter Baker, "Trump Calls Emergency, Defying Congress," *New York Times*, Feb. 16, 2019, A1.

29 Michael Wines, and Adam Liptak, "Justice Dept. Reaffirms Goal For the Census," *New York Times*, July 6, 2019, A1.

an erupting volcano on a Caribbean island—"San Mateo" ("The Doomsday Sanction" 2005). The Supes of *The Boys* only leave the U.S. to fight terrorism.

In episode "The Ties That Bind" (2005), we see the Justice League making foreign policy decisions. Factions on another planet are engaging in intrigue. The Martian Manhunter (representing the political will of the league) decides not to intervene, arguing that the league's intervention could result in "A dictator who could eventually threaten Earth." He adds "better to let them fight amongst themselves." Flash decides on his own to intervene. There is no democratic decision-making process (or appeal to elected officials) to decide these foreign policy matters. The episode "A Better World" (2003) involves an alternate reality, where we see the league take total state power, and in so doing establishes an authoritarian/draconian global regime.

Therefore, in *Justice League Unlimited* and *The Boys* we see a world system whereby the public is outside of the framework of political decision-making. In the real-world investment decisions are under the influence of the market (i.e., privately decided). The U.S. foreign policy apparatus is the most insulated aspect of government—with the national security state operating under a veil of secrecy (and misinformation [e.g., Iraq's WMDs]).[30] *The Boys* focuses on the fact that private corporations are incorporated into the national security state ("Nothing Like It in the World"). American elections are no guarantee against tyranny. In *Justice League Unlimited* we see Lex Luther—corporate head and Superman's villainous nemesis—become the leading candidate for the U.S. presidency. (To Luther: "Have you seen the latest polls? You're going to be our next President" ["Question Authority" (2005)].) In the "A Better World" alternative reality, Luther becomes President of the U.S. Today, former President Donald Trump—who seemingly sought to establish a dictatorship by violently overturning the 2020 election[31]—has announced his candidacy for the presidency in 2024. Additionally, much of the U.S.

---

30 John Prados, *The Family Jewels: The CIA, Secrecy, and Presidential Power* (Austin: University of Texas Press, 2013); Mark Mazzetti, "Senate Drops Bid to Report on Drone Use," *New York Times* April 29, 2014, A10; Michael P. Colaresi, *Democracy Declassified: The Secrecy Dilemma in National Security* (New York: Oxford University Press, 2014); Geoffroy de Lagasnerie, *The Art of Revolt: Snowden, Assange, Manning* (Stanford: Stanford University Press, 2017); Ralph Engelman, and Carey Shenkman, *A Century of Repression: The Espionage Act and Freedom of the Press* (Urbana: University of Illnois Press, 2022).
31 Peter Baker, "Increasingly Unhinged as Power Slipped Away." *New York Times*, June 29, 2022, A1, and "Trump Intent Out in Open." *New York Times*, July 4, 2022, A1.

Republican Party—and its nominees for public office—manifest antipathy toward elections.[32]

Wealth Inequality

The presentation of globalism in *Justice League* highlights the severe economic inequalities which are embedded in the world system. The episode "Twilight" (2003) posits two vastly different planets, "New Genesis" and "Apokolips". Residents of New Genesis appear as highly affluent, whereas the bulk of the inhabitants of Apokolips are very poor (wearing ragged clothes) and enslaved. The planet of New Genesis is beautiful, with lush greenery and a splendid urban environment—a city floating in the sky ("Such Grandeur. I've never seen the like"). Apokolips is hellish—with virtually the entirety of the planet a barren, fiery red (also see "Alive!" [2006]). The leader of Apokolips is the villain "Darkseid" (pronounced Dark-side).

Superman and the Martian Manhunter (J'onn J'onzz) are captured and taken to a peripheral planet (i.e., very distant from Earth)—"War World" (episode title—2002). The planet is ruled by a strong man, or dictator, named

---

32 Reid J. Epstein, and Nick Corasaniti, "They Claim Voter Fraud, Unless It's a G.O.P. Primary," *New York Times*, June 1, 2022, A15; Alexandra Berzon, "2020 Deniers Gain in Races To Run Voting," *New York Times*, June 6, 2022, A1; Azi Paybarah, "Texas G.O.P. Adopts Stolen Election Claims," *New York Times*, June 20, 2022, A13; Stuart A. Thompson, "Right-Wing Radio Sows Doubt About a Vote Yet to Take Place," *New York Times*, July 5, 2022, A1; Nick Corasaniti, "Justice Dept. Sues Arizona Over Voting Law," *New York Times*, July 6, 2022, A15; Editorial Board, "This Threat to Democracy Is Hiding in Plain Sight," Sept. 25, 2022, SR9; Annie Karni, "Far-Right Republicans Face Tough Races in Swing Districts, Testing McCarthy," *New York Times*, Oct. 16, 2022, A29; Robert Draper, "The Problem of Marjorie Taylor Greene," *New York Times Magazine*, Oct. 23, 2022, p. 20; Alexandra Berzon, and Nick Corasaniti, "Right Prepares Activist Army To Watch Vote," *New York Times*, Oct. 18, 2022, A1; Nick Corasaniti, Michael C. Bender, Ruth Igielnik, and Kristen Bayrakdarian, "Most Voters Say U.S. Democracy Is Under Threat," *New York Times*, Oct. 18, 2022, A1; Jonathan Weisman, "Fears Over Fate of Democracy Leave Voters Feeling Defeated," *New York Times*, Oct. 23, 2022, A1; Chris Cameron, "Election Monitors Warning About Republican Deniers," *New York Times*, Oct. 28, 2022, A15; Nick Corasaniti, "As in 2020, Early Election Night Results May Be Misleading Again," *New York Times*, Oct. 28, 2022, A20; Nick Corasaniti, and Alexandra Berzon, "Right-Wing Push For Voting Limits Avoids Spotlight," *New York Times*, May 9, 2023, A1; Shane Goldmacher, Jonathan Swan, Maggie Haberman, and Stephanie Lai, "Trump Lays Out 2nd-Term Vision: Wrecking Norms," *New York Times*, May 12, 2023, A1.

"Mongul", and he oversees gladiatorial games meant to distract the public from the social/economic misery that predominates War World.

> To Mongul: Our nation's food rations is being cut another 15 percent, and then there are the medical shortages and the power blackouts... People are already starting to talk about...
>
> Mongul interjects: Rebellion? There's not going to be any rebellion... Not if I can keep giving them fights. Good ones—enough to take their minds off their troubles.

J'onn walks among crowd attending the games. He asks one woman "So many spectators. Don't they have families or jobs to tend to?" She responds: "Are you kidding? There's no jobs. I haven't worked in years." J'onn: "That's dreadful."

The Boys does not comment directly on wealth inequality—although Vought is a multi-billion dollar corporation. Nevertheless, Supes focus their heroism solely on fighting crime and terrorism. Thus, the political response to poverty and political discontent is repression and vilification. In the television series *Blue Bloods* (2009—) a teacher in an impoverished section of New York City observes about her students that "I can't save all of them or even most of them. But every year I spot one or two.... Kids I can help. Kids who want a shot at a decent life." As for the rest of the students, the seeming response is repression—police detective: "we can't change this neighborhood... [but we can] show these other students that gang violence won't be tolerated in this school" ("School of Hard Knocks" 2018). In the real world, the poor and entire ethnic groups are vilified as criminals or terrorists. Former U.S. President Donald J. Trump based his government on expressly racist policies and rhetoric—condemning Muslims and the poor undocumented. His administration instituted a racist immigration policy of refusing entry to the U.S. of all citizens from a number of Islamic-majority countries.[33] Trump, himself, has issued blanket vilifications of undocumented immigrants (especially from Latin America)—casting them as criminal elements ("rapists", "animals") and an inherent threat to public safety.[34]

---

33 Michael D. Shear, "Trump Imposes New Travel Ban on 7 Countries," *New York Times*, Sept. 25, 2017, A1.
34 Alexander Burns, "Pushing Someone Rich, Trump Offers Himself," *New York Times*, June 17, 2015, A16; also see David Leonhardt, "Trump Encourages Violence," *New York Times*, Mar. 18, 2019, A23.

Neoliberalism

Justice League (*Unlimited*) offers critiques of the neoliberal values that currently predominate in the global economic/political system. The action in "Metamorphosis" (2002) begins with an explosion at an oil drilling site. The next scene shows Simon Stagg, head of Stagg Enterprises, proposing to oil industry executives "Metamorpho"—"a chemically altered worker who will not merely survive in hazardous environments, but will thrive in them." Stagg proposes Metamorpho as a cost saving measure because as a result of "unsafe conditions" "unions are demanding higher wages" and "insurance companies won't cover your risk." The oil company executives do not object to Stagg's proposal for moral reasons. Instead, they don't think his idea is feasible: "I'll believe it when I see it, but not until then." Stagg, without his knowledge, converts his security executive, Rex Mason, into Metamorpho. After seeing video footage of Metamorpho in action against the Justice League, the head of the oil company (Mr. Braddock) calls Stagg.

> Stagg: Is Metamorpho everything I promised?
> Braddock: Everything and more Simon. We want him.
> Stagg: I thought you would. Let's set up a meeting for next week and bring your check book.

Stagg hangs up and declares "A toast to unbridled capitalism!"

Under the present neoliberal regime, workers worldwide are more and more reduced to purely factors of production. Neoliberalism has unleashed a race to the bottom. Countries compete to offer multi-national companies the cheapest (regulation free) platforms of production.[35] We see hundred-of-millions of laborers in China, for instance, working very long hours, for little pay, and no workplace government regulation to speak of.[36] The idea of employers

---

35   Alan Tonelson, *The Race To The Bottom* (New York: Basic Books, 2002); Gérard Duménil, and Dominique Lévy, *Capital Resurgent: Roots of the Neoliberal Revolution*, trans. Derek Jeffers (Cambridge, MA: Harvard University Press, 2004); William I. Robinson, *A Theory of Global Capitalism: Production, Class, and State in a Transnational World* (Baltimore: Johns Hopkins University Press, 2004).

36   Kelly Sims Gallagher, *China Shifts Gears: Automakers, Oil, Pollution, and Development* (Cambridge, MA: MIT Press, 2006); Mary Elizabeth Gallagher, *Contagious Capitalism: Globalization and the Politics of Labor in China* (Princeton: Princeton University Press, 2005); Charles Duhigg, and David Barboza, "In China, the Human Costs That Are Built Into an iPad," *New York Times*, Jan. 26, 2012, A1.

chemically altering workers is far-fetched—nevertheless, it does reflect the virtual absolute power of corporate elites.

The core critique of the *The Boys* is that neoliberalist global capitalism has resulted in corporations having absolute power. Vought is beyond regulation, government oversight. Even when it is exposed that the corporation gave a dangerous serum to infants (to create Supes), it is given a free pass—as the danger from "super villains" trumps this outrage. Under the global neoliberalist regime, the state serves capital, major corporations[37]– as communities, governments are reduced to attracting, maintaining investment by appeasing investors.[38] Public health, education, environmental protection, etc. are transactional as a result.[39]

American Militarism

A particular tension in the current world system is that globalization is changing political power throughout the world. As wealth and power becomes more global (i.e., diffuse), the power/wealth of nation-states declines relative to the world system. In the case of the U.S., the center of the world's industry is shifting away from America and toward the *developing world* (e.g., China).[40] Indicative of the profound imbalance in the present world system is the fact that the U.S. is the nation with the largest defense budget—with less than 5 percent of the world's population it accounts for 40 percent of total global military

---

37 Timothy J. Sinclair, *The New Masters of Capital: American Bond Rating Agencies and the Politics of Creditworthiness* (Ithaca: Cornell University Press, 2014); Clyde W. Barrow, *Toward a Critical Theory of States: The Poulantzas-Miliband Debate After Globalization* (Albany: State University of New York Press, 2016); William Deringer, *Calculated Values: Finance, Politics, and the Quantitative Age* (Cambridge, MA: Harvard University Press, 2018).
38 Layna Mosley, *Global Capital and National Governments* (Cambridge: Cambridge University Press, 2003); Nick Wingfield, and Patricia Cohen, "Let the Bidding Begin," *New York Times*, Sept. 8, 2017, B1; François Chesnais, *Finance Capital Today: Corporations and Banks in the Lasting Global Slump* (Chicago: Haymarket Books, 2018).
39 Jane L. Collins, and Victoria Mayer, *Both Hands Tied: Welfare Reform and the Race to the Bottom in the Low-Wage Labor Market* (Chicago: University of Chicago Press, 2010); Kristin S. Seefedt, and John D. Graham, *America's Poor and the Great Recession* (Bloomington: Indiana University Press, 2013); George A. Gonzalez, *Energy, the Modern State, and the American World System* (Albany: State University of New York Press, 2018).
40 David Shambaugh, *China Goes Global: The Partial Power* (Oxford University Press, 2013).

expenditures.[41] In the recent past the U.S. spent more on its military than the rest of the world combined.[42] The U.S. (by far) also has the largest trade[43] and public debt in the world[44]—with the American government alone owing trillions of dollars to China and Japan.[45]

Justice League Unlimited indicates that the burst of American militarism (invasions of faraway countries, as well as the use of torture) in the 2000s is an effort to combat geopolitical decline in response to economic/political globalization. This militarism is prompting greater secrecy; less democracy; and more authoritarianism. "Cadmus" is formed—a secret U.S. government agency to counter the Justice League (read globalization). Cadmus is involved in "secret weapons; illegal cloning experiments; bypassing Congress" ("The Doomsday Sanction"). It is referred to as "a shadow cabinet" and "a black ops group"—with "legitimate connections to the government" ("Flashpoint"). Cadmus, in another instance, is described as a collection of "power brokers, politicians, criminals, and black ops mercenaries" ("Question Authority")—as the Blackwater security outfit, which works closely with the U.S. military and intelligence agencies, might be described.[46] The head of Cadmus "served in intelligence under three Administrations" ("The Doomsday Sanction"). The U.S. President orders a Cadmus assault on the league's Watchtower ("Question Authority").

---

41 SIPRI. *SIPRI Fact Sheet: Trends in World Military Expenditure, 2021* (Stockholm: SIPRI, April 2022). Web.
42 Matt Moore, "Global Military Spending Soars," Associated Press, June 9, 2004. Web; Edward S. Greenberg, and Benjamin I. Page, *The Struggle for Democracy*, 7th ed. (New York: Pearson Longman, 2004), 545; Thom Shanker, "Proposed Military Spending Is Highest Since WWII," *New York Times*, Feb. 4, 2008, A10; Andrew Cockburn, *The Spoils of War: Power, Profit and the American War Machine* (New York: Verso, 2021).
43 "Trade Deficit Narrow, Countering Report of a Contraction," *New York Times*, Feb. 9, 2013, B6; Matthew C. Klein, and Michael Pettis, *Trade Wars Are Class Wars: How Rising Inequality Distorts the Global Economy and Threatens International Peace* (New Haven: Yale University Press, 2020); Ana Swanson, "U.S. Trade Deficit Surged In 2022, Nearing $1 Trillion," *New York Times*, Feb. 8, 2023, B3.
44 Alan Rappeport, and Jim Tankersley, "U.S. Debt Surpasses $31 Trillion," *New York Times*, Oct. 5, 2022, B1.
45 David Barboza, "China's Treasury Holdings Make U.S. Woes its Own," *New York Times*, July 19, 2011, B1.
46 Suzanne Simons, *Master of War: Blackwater USA's Erik Prince and the Business of War* (New York: Harper, 2009); James Risen, and Mark Mazetti, "Case Ends Against Ex-Blackwater Officials," *New York Times*, Feb. 22, 2013, A16.

Cadmus works in alliance with Lex Luther, head of Lex Corp.—a wealthy corporation. Luther captures league member The Question and turns him over to Cadmus—where he is tortured with electric shocks ("Question Authority"). The Question's only super ability is a critical/forensic mind. The movie *Zero Dark Thirty* (2012) (made in close collaboration with the U.S. military and the Central Intelligence Agency) indicates that torture is used by the U.S. government in its dealings abroad.[47] Additionally, in 2013 the *New York Times* reported that "A nonpartisan, independent review of interrogation and detention programs in the years after the Sept. 11, 2001, terrorist attacks concludes that 'it is indisputable that the United States engaged in the practice of torture' and that the nation's highest officials bore ultimate responsibility for it."[48] Moreover, the U.S. government controls "black sites" throughout the world where torture may occur.[49]

The contemporary wanton violence of the U.S. national security state is represented in "The Doomsday Sanction" when the military launches a nuclear missile that would kill everyone (including innocent residents) on a Caribbean Island.

> To General Eiling: What were you thinking [launching a nuclear missile]? You're going to kill Superman and everyone else on the island.
>
> General Eiling: We have to sanction Doomsday [a Cadmus weapon run amok]. We were going to get to Superman somewhere down the line. And we've been trying to stop drug traffic from San Mateo for years. The way I see it—three birds, one stone.

The *New York Times* notes that the George W. Bush Administration "reserved the right to use nuclear weapons 'to deter a wide range of threats.'"[50]

---

47 Scott Shane, "C.I.A.'s History Poses Hurdles for an Obama Nominee," *New York Times*, Mar. 7, 2012, A1, and "Portrayal of C.I.A. Torture in Bin Laden Film Reopens a Debate," *New York Times* Dec. 13, 2012, A1.

48 Scott Shane, "U.S. Practiced Torture After 9/11, Nonpartisan Review Concludes," *New York Times*, Apr. 16, 2013, A1; also see Mark Mazzetti, "Panel Faults C.I.A. Over Brutality Toward Terrorism Suspects," *New York Times*, Dec. 10, 2014, A1; Carol Rosenberg, "War Crimes Hearing Revisits Abuses Meted by U.S. Troops," *New York Times*, May 2, 2022, A8, "Psychologist Describes Fearing for Prisoner at C.I.A. Black Site," *New York Times*, May 4, 2022, A22, "Court Re-enacts C.I.A. Interrogation Tactics," *New York Times*, Apr. 14, 2023, A18, and "Red Cross Sounds Alarm Over Health Of Detainees," *New York Times*, Apr. 22, 2023, A16.

49 Editorial Board, "About Those Black Sites," *New York Times*, Feb. 18, 2013, A16.

50 As quoted in David E. Sanger, and Peter Baker, "Obama Limits When U.S. Would Use Nuclear Arms," *New York Times*, Apr. 6, 2010, A1.

Justice League Unlimited episode "Patriot Act" (2006), more so than any other instantiation of U.S. popular culture, depicts the argument that contemporary American militarism and wanton global violence are a direct response to U.S. decline resulting from globalization. Cadmus has been disbanded, as has its weapon program. Its former head, General Wade Eilings holds that the U.S. needs the weapons that Cadmus was overseeing to protect against the Justice League (again, read globalization), and decides to take matters into his own hands. The General breaks into a military facility where an experimental Nazi serum is held. The serum was developed to create a "Captain Nazi"—a counter to Captain America. The General injects himself with the serum, and it turns him into a huge hideous grayish muscular monster—with super powers. He seeks out the Justice League for a violent showdown. The General exclaims "Your Justice League [is] a threat to a safe and stable world." The Justice League is the reason that "this country is half way down the toilet." The General proclaims "I'll waste you and a billion like you before I let any power rival America's—It's my duty."[51]

Mila Bongco, in her 2000 literary criticism of comic book heroes, describes their historical transformation: "Since the early the 1970s, they have been shown routing out scientists, politicians, priests, and other establishment figures who turn out to be in league with criminal elements.[52] *Justice League Unlimited*, with episodes like "The Doomsday Sanction", "Question Authority", and "Patriot Act," has gone further than simply suggesting that particular individuals, or groups of individuals, are misusing (government) authority/resources. Instead, the claim is being made that the American state in the 2000s is out of control and fundamentally dangerous.

Conclusion

Marc DiPaolo, in his important book, *War, Politics and Superheroes*, outlines how "politically themed superhero adventures tend to fall into three different

---

51 In 2002, President George W. Bush stated: "We must build and maintain our defenses beyond challenge." "Our forces will be strong enough to dissuade potential adversaries from pursuing a military build-up in hopes of surpassing, or equaling, the power of the United States." "Full Text: Bush's National Security Strategy," *New York Times*, Sept. 20, 2002. Web; *The National Security Strategy of the United States of America* (Washington, DC: The White House, Sept. 2002), 29–30.

52 Mila Bongco, *Reading Comics: Language, Culture, and the Concept of the Superhero in Comic Books* (New York: Garland, 2000), 93–94.

categories: establishment, anti-establishment, and colonial."[53] While *Justice League* (*Unlimited*) could be categorized as anti-establishment (or adopting a critical tone toward existing values and policies), my view is this television series transcends simply taking a negative tack on dominate attitudes and state actions. Instead, *Justice League Unlimited* can be readily cast as "political art"—i.e., giving viewers analytical insight into present-day world politics, as well as global conceptions of (in)justice.[54] A similar point can made with *The Boys*—a precise, unflinching critique of corporate power.

More specifically, the Justice League, in *Justice League Unlimited*, is symbolic of globalization, with the league reflecting the need for world (justice) government (e.g., responding to crises throughout the planet). The fact that the league operates from space (i.e., the Watchtower)—outside of the nation-state system—strongly indicates it is a metaphor for the current globalizing of political and economic power. Interpreting *Justice League Unlimited* as a commentary on the politics of the world system allows us to read the show as rendering critical observations/meditations on democracy (the lack thereof), wealth inequality, neoliberalism, and American militarism. Ultimately, *Justice League Unlimited* indicates that the absence of democracy; glaring wealth inequality; and neoliberalism are combining into increasing and dangerous American militarism (injustice).

For its part, *The Boys* is an overt, incisive satirizing of the Nationalist Superhero, and of the injustice of corporate power within the context of neoliberalist global capitalism. As such, *The Boys* deepens the analysis put forward in *Justice League Unlimited*. It specifically puts forth the idea that corporate dominance is even more entrenched and American global violence has become more routinized and even less transparent since the first decade of the 21st century.

---

53 Marc DiPaolo, *War, Politics and Superheroes* (London: McFarland, 2013), 12.
54 Jacques Rancière, *Aesthetics and Its Discontents*, trans. Steve Corcoran (Malden, MA: Polity, 2009); George A. Gonzalez, *Justice and Popular Culture: Star Trek as Philosophical Text* (Lanham, MD: Lexington Books, 2019), and *Popular Culture as Art and Knowledge* (Lanham, MD: Lexington Books, 2019); Robert B. Pippin, *Philosophy by Other Means: The Arts in Philosophy and Philosophy in the Arts* (Chicago: University of Chicago Press, 2021).

Conclusion

POPULAR CULTURE AS PRIME POLITICAL TERRAIN IN THE STRUGGLE FOR DEMOCRACY/JUSTICE

The *New York Times* in September of 2022 acknowledged the institutional threat the U.S. Republican Party, under the leadership of former President Donald J. Trump, poses to American democracy.[1] What the *New York Times* does not note is that the Democratic Party is abetting this ongoing conspiracy[2] insofar as the Democratic presidential administration of Joe Biden (2021–) has failed to charge Trump[3] for his well-documented role in the Jan. 6th

---

1 David Leonhardt, "Democracy Challenged," *New York Times*, Sept. 18, 2022, A1. See also Editorial Board, "How a G.O.P. Faction Enables Political Violence," *New York Times*, Nov. 27, 2022, SR9.
2 Jamelle Bouie, "The Trump Conspiracy Is Hiding in Plain Sight," *New York Times*, Dec. 5, 2021, SR7; Maggie Haberman, Alexandra Berzon, and Michael S. Schmidt, "Trump's Allies Keep Up Fight To Nullify Vote," *New York Times*, Apr. 19, 2022, A1; Adam Liptak, and Nick Corasaniti, "Supreme Court Could Reshape Election Rules," *New York Times*, July 1, 2022, A1; Reid J. Epstein, "Accept Defeat? Some in G.O.P. Refuse to Say," *New York Times*, Sept. 19, 2022, A1.
3 Glenn Thrush, "Divisions Imperil Democracy, Garland Warns New Citizens," *New York Times*, Sept. 18, 2022, A29, and "Garland Gingerly Steps Outside Comfort Zone With Trump Inquiries," *New York Times*, Nov. 29, 2022, A15; Peter Baker, "Laying Out the 6 Legal Battles Putting Trump at Growing Risk," *New York Times*, Sept. 19, 2022, A1; Luke Broadwater, "Top Staff Investigator Shares Lessons of the House's Jan. 6 Inquiry," *New York Times*, Feb. 20, 2023, A13.

(2021) effort to violently upend the 2020 election[4]—presumably maintaining himself as U.S. president into the foreseeable future (in other words, brutal dictatorship).[5] Trump expressly repudiated the U.S. Constitution in calling for his reinstallation as President,[6] and it is noteworthy that former President Trump consorts with full-throated (purveyors of hate) anti-Semites, white supremacists.[7] Trump – through the online platform of Truth Social – personally promotes the hate fostering political fantasies of QAnon.[8] Elsewhere I have argued that authoritarianism and hate-mongering are targeted against the *progressive dialectic*—the evolution of humanity toward a modern classless society, totally free of ethnic, gender biases.[9]

---

4 Peter Baker, "Increasingly Unhinged as Power Slipped Away," *New York Times*, June 29, 2022, A1, and "Trump Intent Out in Open," *New York Times*, July 4, 2022, A1. Trump in August 2023 was charged by the U.S. Justice Department with falsely claiming he won the 2020 election and for trying to retain the Presidency through illegal bureaucratic maneuvers. Importantly, former President Trump was not indicted for his role in the deadly Jan. 6th (2021) ransacking of Congress (the Capitol Building). Alan Feuer, and Maggie Haberman, "Trump Charged With 'Destabilizing Lies' in 3 Conspiracies to Overturn His Defeat," *New York Times*, Aug. 2, 2023, A1; Michael S. Schmidt, and Maggie Haberman, "First Amendment is Likely Linchpin of Trump Defense," *New York Times*, Aug. 3, 2023, A1.
5 The *New York Times* reported the following: "Mr. Trump posted an image of himself on Truth Social, wearing a Q pin on his lapel and under a slogan reading 'The Storm is Coming.' Adherents to QAnon believe that the 'storm' is the moment when Mr. Trump will retake power after vanquishing his enemies, having them arrested and potentially executed on live TV." Alan Feuer, and Maggie Haberman, "At Trump Rally, Crowd Reacts to QAnon-Like Music," *New York Times*, Sept. 19, 2022, A14.
6 Maggie Astor, "Trump's Call To Suspend Constitution Gets Rebukes," *New York Times*, Dec. 5, 2022, A13.
7 Maggie Haberman, and Alan Feuer, "Invited Over to Trump's, an Outcast Rapper Brings Along a White Supremacist," *New York Times*, Nov. 26, 2022, A20; Jonathan Weisman, "Jewish Allies of Trump Recoil After He Hosts 2 Antisemites," *New York Times*, Nov. 29, 2022, A1.
8 Ken Bensinger, and Maggie Haberman, "Trump Postings During His Ban Tilted Far Right," *New York Times*, Jan. 29, 2023, A1. The *New York Times* reports that "QAnon is the umbrella term for a set of internet conspiracy theories [fantasies] that allege the world is run by a cabal of Satan-worshiping pedophiles." Kevin Roose, "What Is QAnon, the Conspiracy Swarm?" *New York Times*, Aug. 19, 2020, B1.
9 George A. Gonzalez, *Justice and Popular Culture: Star Trek as Philosophical Text* (Lanham, MD: Lexington Books, 2019), and *Popular Culture, Conspiracy Theory, and the Star Trek Text* (Lanham, MD, Lexington Books, 2020). Also see Alexandra Alter, and Elizabeth A. Harris, "Attempts to Ban Books Are Increasing," *New York Times*, Sept. 17, 2022, C2.

In *Star Trek and Popular Culture: Television at the Frontier of Social, Political Change in the 1960s* I explain that popular culture is a key aspect of democracy—insofar as the values of the 60s revolution are disseminated by popular culture.[10] Put differently, American movies and television shows—to the extent that they attain a worldwide audience—make feminism, civil rights, gender (LGBTQ), and ethnic fairness a salient aspect of society, culture.

At the core of the philosophy of entertainment is the *spirit of justice*—justice animating scripts, actors, production values and vice versa (justice brought to life). This is evident (in the negative) with Nazi cinema (1940s) (Chapter 2), American *outer space* science fiction movies of the McCarthy era (the 1950s) (Chapter 3), and popular culture during the American war in Vietnam (1965–1973) (Chapter 2). In each of these cases popular culture could not be used to put colonial war, demeaning (degrading) hate, nor repression in a positive light.

While authoritarian regimes cannot use popular culture to promote backward, repressive politics, such regimes can stop popular culture from serving to forward the *progressive dialectic*. Notably, even as the American military was engaged in a brutal war in Vietnam to suppress a movement against colonialism (white supremacy) the creators of *Star Trek* were openly criticizing the war (Chapter 2), as well as arguing against white supremacy, patriarchy, and for global solidarity (Chapter 4).

The creators of the Star Trek franchise have been engaged in a project of depicting justice for close to 60 years (Chapters 4 and 5)—accounting for the franchise's continuing, immense popularity. The *Justice League Unlimited* indicates that globalism (world government) is the only form of justice that is rational in a global economy, society. *The Boys* outlines the destructive, authoritarian pathologies (injustice) of global corporate power (Chapter 6). Popular culture playing the role of conveying, exploring, analyzing justice is a prime aspect of a democratic polity. In other words, a vital component of democracy is the engagement of the Enlightenment (the *progressive dialectic*) via popular culture.[11] Arguably, this would be the most visible aspect of democracy lost in a (Trump, Republican) dictatorship.

---

10 George A. Gonzalez, *Star Trek and Popular Culture: Television at the Frontier of the Social, Political Change in the 1960s* (New York: Peter Lang, 2021).

11 George A. Gonzalez, *Star Trek and Star Wars: The Enlightenment versus the Anti-Enlightenment* (New York: Peter Lang, 2022).

BIBLIOGRAPHY

"A Special Weekly Report from the Wall Street Journal's Capital Bureau." *Wall Street Journal*, October 27, 1967, p. 1.

Alexander, David. *Star Trek Creator: The Authorized Biography of Gene Roddenberry*. New York: Penguin Books, 1994.

Alter, Alexandra, and Elizabeth A. Harris. "Attempts to Ban Books Are Increasing." *New York Times*, September 17, 2022, C2.

Anderson, Terry H. *Bush's Wars*. New York: Oxford University Press, 2011.

Astor, Maggie. "Elizabeth Warren, Criticizing Bloomberg, Sent a Message: She Won't Be Ignored." *New York Times*, February 19, 2020, Web.

Astor, Maggie. "Trump's Call To Suspend Constitution Gets Rebukes." *New York Times*, December 5, 2022, A13.

Bachrach, Susan, and Steven Luckert. *State of Deception: The Power of Nazi Propaganda*. Washington, DC: U.S. Holocaust Memorial Museum, 2009.

Baker, Peter. "Trump's Insults End a Brief Civil Interlude." *New York Times*, Dec. 8, 2018, A10.

Baker, Peter. "Trump Calls Emergency, Defying Congress." *New York Times*, February 16, 2019, A1.

Baker, Peter. "Increasingly Unhinged as Power Slipped Away." *New York Times*, June 29, 2022, A1.

Baker, Peter. "Trump Intent Out in Open." *New York Times*, July 4, 2022, A1.

Baker, Peter. "Laying Out the 6 Legal Battles Putting Trump at Growing Risk." *New York Times*, September 19, 2022, A1.

Baker, Peter, Lisa Friedman, and Christopher Flavelle. "At Odds with Scientists, Trump Intervened to 'Clarify' Forecasts." *New York Times*, September 12, 2019, A1.

Barboza, David. "China's Treasury Holdings Make U.S. Woes Its Own." *New York Times*, July 19, 2011, B1.

Barilleaux, Ryan J., and Christopher S. Kelley, eds. *The Unitary Executive and the Modern Presidency*. College Station: Texas A&M University Press, 2010.

Barrow, Clyde W. *Toward a Critical Theory of States: The Poulantzas-Miliband Debate After Globalization*. Albany: State University of New York Press, 2016.

Belew, Kathleen. *Bring the War Home: The White Power Movement and Paramilitary America*. Cambridge, MA: Harvard University Press, 2018.

Belew, Kathleen. "Militant Whiteness in the Age of Trump." In *The Presidency of Donald J. Trump: A First Historical Assessment*, ed. Julian E. Zelizer. Princeton: Princeton University Press, 2022.

Belson, Ken, and Jenny Vrentas. "After Investigation, Snyder Faces $60 Million Fine." *New York Times*, July 21, 2023, B8.

Belson, Ken, and Katherine Rosman. "Congress Slams N.F.L. and the Owner of the Washington Commanders." *New York Times*, December 9, 2022, B7.

Belson, Ken, and Katherine Rosman. "Snyder Agrees to Sell Commanders for $6 Billion." *New York Times*, April 14, 2023, B6.

Benner, Katie. "Legal Opinions Support Executive Privilege." *New York Times*, December 13, 2019, A17.

Bensinger, Ken, and Maggie Haberman. "Trump Postings During His Ban Tilted Far Right." *New York Times*, January 29, 2023, A1.

Berkowitz, Eric. *Dangerous Ideas: A Brief History of Censorship in the West, from the Ancients to Fake News*. Boston: Beacon Press, 2021.

Bernardi, Daniel Leonard. *Star Trek and History: Race-ing toward a White Future*. New Brunswick, NJ: Rutgers University Press, 1998.

Berzon, Alexandra. "2020 Deniers Gain in Races To Run Voting." *New York Times*, June 6, 2022, A1.

Berzon, Alexandra, and Nick Corasaniti. "Right Prepares Activist Army To Watch Vote." *New York Times*, October 18, 2022.

Beschloss, Michael R. *Mayday: Eisenhower, Khrushchev, and the U-2 Affair*. New York: Harper and Row, 1988.

Bindas, Kenneth J. *Modernity and the Great Depression: The Transformation of American Society, 1930–1941*. Lawrence: University Press of Kansas, 2017.

Blackford, Russell. *Science Fiction and the Moral Imagination: Visions, Minds, Ethics*. Cham, DEN: Springer Publishing, 2017.

Blow, Charles M. "An Imperial Presidency?" *New York Times*, May 13, 2019, A19.

Blow, Charles M. "Whitewashing White Nationalism." *New York Times*, July 16, 2023, SR3.

Bongco, Mila. *Reading Comics: Language, Culture, and the Concept of the Superhero in Comic Books*. New York: Garland, 2000.

Bouie, Jamelle. "The Trump Conspiracy Is Hiding in Plain Sight." *New York Times*, December 5, 2021, SR7.

Brandom, Robert B. *A Spirit of Trust: A Reading of Hegel's Phenomenology*. Cambridge, MA: Belknap, 2019.
Brice-Saddler, Michael. "While Bemoaning Mueller Probe, Trump Falsely Says the Constitution Gives Him 'the right to do whatever I want'." *Washington Post*, July 23, 2019. Web.
Broadwater, Luke. "Top Staff Investigator Shares Lessons of the House's Jan. 6 Inquiry." *New York Times*, February 20, 2023, A13.
Broadwater, Luke, and Maggie Haberman. "Trump Reply To Congress Repeats Lies On Election." *New York Times*, October 15, 2022, A17.
Bronner, Stephen Eric. *Rosa Luxemburg: A Revolutionary for Our Times*. University Park: Pennsylvania State University Press, 1993.
Brooks, Tim, and Earle Marsh. *The Complete Directory to Prime Time Network and Cable TV Shows 1946–Present*. Twentieth Anniversary ed. New York: Ballantine Books, 1999.
Burns, Alexander. "Pushing Someone Rich, Trump Offers Himself." *New York Times*, June 17, 2015, A16.
Burns, Alexander, Jonathan Martin, and Maggie Haberman. "Trump Escalates Push to Erode Trust in Vote." *New York Times*, October 1, 2020, A1.
Burns, Tony. "Marxism vs. Postmodernism: The Case of *The Matrix*." In *Red Alert: Marxist Approaches to Science Fiction Cinema*, ed. Ewa Mazierska and Alfredo Suppia. Detroit: Wayne State University Press, 2016.
Bytwerk, Randall L. *Bending Spines: The Propagandas of Nazi Germany and the German Democratic Republic*. Lansing: Michigan State University Press, 2004.
Cameron, Chris. "Election Monitors Warning About Republican Deniers." *New York Times*, October 28, 2022, A15.
Campbell, Gordon, ed. *The Oxford Illustrated History of the Renaissance*. New York: Oxford University Press, 2019.
Capaldi, Nicholas. *The Enlightenment Project in the Analytic Conversation*. Boston: Kluwer Academic Publishers, 1998.
Carrington, André M. *Speculative Blackness: The Future of Race in Science Fiction*. Minneapolis: University of Minnesota Press, 2016.
Carter, Dan T. *The Politics of Rage: George Wallace, the Origins of the New Conservatism, and the Transformation of American Politics*, 2nd ed. Baton Rouge: Louisiana State University, 2000.
Carwardine, Richard, and Jay Sexton, eds. *The Global Lincoln*. New York: Oxford University Press, 2011.
Chesnais, François. *Finance Capital Today: Corporations and Banks in the Lasting Global Slump*. Chicago: Haymarket Books, 2018.
Childs, Peter. *Modernism*, 3rd ed. New York: Routledge, 2016.
Claridge, Laura. *Emily Post: Daughter of the Gilded Age, Mistress of American Manners*. New York: Random House, 2009.
Cochrane, Emily. "A Passive Congress Enables Trump to Use Pulpit to Continue His Shutdown Chatter." *New York Times*, December 25, 2018, A15.
Cockburn, Andrew. *The Spoils of War: Power, Profit and the American War Machine*. New York: Verso, 2021.

Colaresi, Michael P. *Democracy Declassified: The Secrecy Dilemma in National Security.* New York: Oxford University Press, 2014.

Collins, Jane L., and Victoria Mayer. *Both Hands Tied: Welfare Reform and the Race to the Bottom in the Low-Wage Labor Market.* Chicago: University of Chicago Press, 2010.

Committee on Oversight and Reform (U.S. House of Representatives). *Conduct Detrimental: How the NFL and the Washington Commanders Covered Up Decades of Sexual Misconduct.* Washington, DC: Government Printing Office, December 8, 2022.

Coontz, Stephanie. *Marriage, a History: From Obedience to Intimacy, or How Love Conquered Marriage.* New York: Viking, 2005.

Corasaniti, Nick. "Justice Dept. Sues Arizona Over Voting Law." *New York Times*, July 6, 2022, A15.

Corasaniti, Nick. "As in 2020, Early Election Night Results May Be Misleading Again." *New York Times*, October 28, 2022, A20.

Corasaniti, Nick, and Alexandra Berzon. "Right-Wing Push For Voting Limits Avoids Spotlight." *New York Times*, May 9, 2023, A1.

Corasaniti, Nick, Michael C. Bender, Ruth Igielnik, and Kristen Bayrakdarian. "Most Voters Say U.S. Democracy Is Under Threat." *New York Times*, October 18, 2022, A1.

Daddis, Gregory A. *Westmoreland's War: Reassessing American Strategy in Vietnam.* New York: Oxford University Press, 2014.

Daddis, Gregory A. *Withdrawal: Reassessing America's Final Years in Vietnam.* New York: Oxford University Press, 2017.

Davey, Monica. "A Picture of Detroit Ruin, Street by Forlorn Street." *New York Times*, February 18, 2014, A1.

de Lagasnerie, Geoffroy. *The Art of Revolt: Snowden, Assange, Manning.* Stanford: Stanford University Press, 2017.

Deringer, William. *Calculated Values: Finance, Politics, and the Quantitative Age.* Cambridge, MA: Harvard University Press, 2018.

Desmond, William. *Art and the Absolute: A Study of Hegel's Aesthetics.* Albany: State University of New York Press, 1986.

Dierenfield, Bruce J. *The Civil Rights Movement*, rev. ed. New York: Routledge, 2014.

DiPaolo, Marc. *War, Politics and Superheroes.* London: McFarland, 2013.

Dittmar, Linda, and Gene Michaud. "America's Vietnam War Films: Marching toward Denial." In *From Hanoi to Hollywood: The Vietnam War in American Film*, ed. Linda Dittmar and Gene Michaud. New Brunswick, NJ: Rutgers University Press, 1990.

Dittmer, Jason. *Captain America and the Nationalist Superhero.* Philadelphia: Temple University Press, 2012.

Domby, Adam H. *The False Cause: Fraud, Fabrication, and White Supremacy in Confederate Memory.* Charlottesville: University of Virginia Press, 2020.

Downs, Gregory P. *The Second American Revolution: The Civil War-Era Struggle over Cuba and the Rebirth of the American Republic.* Chapel Hill: University of North Carolina Press, 2019.

Doyle, William. *The French Revolution: A Very Short Introduction*, 2nd ed. New York: Oxford University Press, 2020.

BIBLIOGRAPHY

Drape, Joe. "Bankruptcy for Ailing Detroit, but Prosperity for Its Teams." *New York Times*, October 14., 2013, A1.
Draper, Robert. "The Problem of Marjorie Taylor Greene." *New York Times Magazine*, October 23, 2022, p. 20.
Dudley, Will, ed. *Hegel and History*. Albany: State University of New York Press, 2009.
Duhigg, Charles, and David Barboza. "In China, the Human Costs That Are Built Into an iPad." *New York Times*, January 26, 2012, A1.
Duménil, Gérard, and Dominique Lévy. *Capital Resurgent: Roots of the Neoliberal Revolution*, trans. Derek Jeffers. Cambridge, MA: Harvard University Press, 2004.
Editorial Board. "About Those Black Sites." *New York Times*, February 18, 2013, A16.
Editorial Board. "Why Does the U.S. Military Celebrate White Supremacy?" *New York Times*, May 24, 2020, SR8.
Editorial Board. "Ms. Greene Is Beyond the Pale." *New York Times*, February 1, 2021, A20.
Editorial Board. "This Threat to Democracy Is Hiding in Plain Sight." September 25, 2022, SR9.
Editorial Board. "How a G.O.P. Faction Enables Political Violence." *New York Times*, November 27, 2022, SR9.
Editors of History Channel. *History The 1960's*. New York: History Channel, 2019.
Editors of LIFE. *LIFE The 1960s: The Decade When Everything Changed*. New York: LIFE, 2016.
Elias, Christopher M. *Gossip Men: J. Edgar Hoover, Joe McCarthy, Roy Cohn, and the Politics of Insinuation*. Chicago: University of Chicago Press, 2021.
Engelman, Ralph, and Carey Shenkman. *A Century of Repression: The Espionage Act and Freedom of the Press*. Urbana: University of Illinois Press, 2022.
Epstein, Reid J. "Accept Defeat? Some in G.O.P. Refuse to Say." *New York Times*, September 19, 2022, A1.
Epstein, Reid J., and Nick Corasaniti. "They Claim Voter Fraud, Unless It's a G.O.P. Primary." *New York Times*, June 1, 2022, A15.
Fahy, Thomas, ed. *The Philosophy of Horror*. Lexington: University of Kentucky Press, 2012.
Faust, Drew Gilpin. *The Creation of Confederate Nationalism: Ideology and Identity in the Civil War South*. Baton Rouge: Louisiana State University Press, 1988.
Finder, Henry, ed. *The 60s: The Story of a Decade*. New York: New Yorker, 2016.
Feuer, Alan. "A Few Main Characters Form the Core of the Committee's Narrative." *New York Times*, June 10, 2022, A16.
Feuer, Alan. "Gun-Toting Candidate's Ad Suggests Hunt for 'RINOs'." *New York Times*, June 21, 2022, A17.
Feuer, Alan. "Testimony of Trump Allies And Extremists at Hearing." *New York Times*, June 30, 2022, A17.
Feuer, Alan, and Maggie Haberman. "At Trump Rally, Crowd Reacts to QAnon-Like Music." *New York Times*, September 19, 2022, A14.
Feuer, Alan, and Maggie Haberman. "Trump Charged With 'Destabilizing Lies' in 3 Conspiracies to Overturn His Defeat." *New York Times*, Aug. 2, 2023, A1.
Fine, Aaron. *Color Theory: A Critical Introduction*. New York: Bloombury, 2021.
Fischer, Nick. *Spider Web: The Birth of American Anticommunism*. Urbana: University of Illinois Press, 2016.

Flavelle, Christopher, and Lisa Friedman. "President Acts To Undermine Science Agency." *New York Times*, October 28, 2020, A1.

Frankfurt, Harry G. *On Bullshit*. Princeton: Princeton University Press, 2005.

Frölich, Paul. *Rosa Luxemburg: Her Life and Work*. New York: Howard Fertig, 1969.

"Full Text: Bush's National Security Strategy." *New York Times*, September 20, 2002. Web.

Gaddis, John Lewis. *Strategies of Containment: A Critical Appraisal of Postwar American National Security Policy*. New York: Oxford University Press, 1982.

Gallagher, Kelly Sims. *China Shifts Gears: Automakers, Oil, Pollution, and Development*. Cambridge, MA: MIT Press, 2006.

Gallagher, Mary Elizabeth. *Contagious Capitalism: Globalization and the Politics of Labor in China*. Princeton: Princeton University Press, 2005.

Garden, Ian. *The Third Reich's Celluloid War: Propaganda in Nazi Feature Films, Documentaries and Television*. Gloucestershire, UK: History Press, 2015.

Gartman, David. *Culture, Class, and Critical Theory: Between Bourdieu and the Frankfurt School*. New York: Routledge, 2012.

Gentry, Curt. *J. Edgar Hoover: The Man and the Secrets*. New York: Norton, 2001.

Giridharadas, Anand. "Warren Buffett and the Myth of the 'Good Billionaire'." *New York Times*, June 14, 2021, A23.

Giuffre, Katherine. *Outrage: The Arts and the Creation of Modernity*. Stanford: Stanford University Press, 2023.

Glock, Hans-Johann. *What Is Analytic Philosophy?* New York: Cambridge University Press, 2008.

Goldmacher, Shane, Jonathan Swan, Maggie Haberman, and Stephanie Lai. "Trump Lays Out 2nd-Term Vision: Wrecking Norms." *New York Times*, May 12, 2023, A1.

Goldman, Adam, and Shaila Dewan. "Shouting, Smashed Glass, A Lunge, Then a Gunshot." *New York Times*, January 24, 2021, A1.

Gonzalez, George A. *The Politics of Star Trek: Justice, War and the Future*. New York: Palgrave Macmillan, 2015.

Gonzalez, George A. "*Justice League Unlimited* and the Politics of Globalization." *Foundation: The International Review of Science Fiction* 45, no. 123 (2016): 5-13.

Gonzalez, George A. *The Absolute and Star Trek*. New York: Palgrave Macmillan, 2017.

Gonzalez, George A. *Energy, the Modern State, and the American World System*. Albany: State University of New York Press, 2018.

Gonzalez, George A. *Star Trek and the Politics of Globalism*. New York: Palgrave Macmillan, 2018.

Gonzalez, George A. *Justice and Popular Culture: Star Trek as Philosophical Text*. Lanham, MD: Lexington Books, 2019.

Gonzalez, George A. *Popular Culture and the Political Values of Neoliberalism*. Lanham, MD: Lexington Books, 2019.

Gonzalez, George A. *Popular Culture as Art and Knowledge*. Lanham, MD: Lexington Books, 2019.

Gonzalez, George A. *Popular Culture, Conspiracy Theory and the Star Trek Text*. Lanham, MD: Lexington Books, 2020.

Gonzalez, George A. "'May we Together Become Greater': in Defence of Star Trek and Anti-Racism." *Foundation: The International Review of Science Fiction* 50, no. 138 (2021): 14–22.

Gonzalez, George A. *Star Trek and Popular Culture: Television at the Frontier of Social and Political Change in the 1960s*. New York: Peter Lang, 2021.

Gonzalez, George A. *Star Trek and Star Wars: The Enlightenment versus the Anti-Enlightenment*. New York: Peter Lang, 2022.

Goodman, Peter S. "U.S. and Global Economies Slipping in Unison." *New York Times*, August 24, 2008, A1.

Goodman, Peter S. *Davos Man: How the Billionaires Devoured the World*. New York: Custom House, 2022.

Goodwin, Richard N. *Remembering America: A Voice from the Sixties*. Boston: Little, Brown, 1988.

Graziano, Michael. *Errand Into the Wilderness of Mirrors*. Chicago: University of Chicago Press, 2021.

Greenberg, Edward S., and Benjamin I. Page. *The Struggle for Democracy*, 7th ed. New York: Pearson Longman, 2004.

Greven, David. *Gender and Sexuality in Star Trek: Allegories of Desire in the Television Series and Films*. Jefferson, NC: MacFarland, 2009.

Gross, Daniel A. "'Deutschland über Alles' and 'America First,' in Song." *New Yorker*, February 18, 2017. Web.

Gutterman, Lauren Jae. *Her Neighbor's Wife: A History of Lesbian Desire within Marriage*. Philadelphia: University of Pennsylvania Press, 2020.

Haberman, Maggie, Alexandra Berzon, and Michael S. Schmidt. "Trump's Allies Keep Up Fight To Nullify Vote." *New York Times*, April 19, 2022, A1.

Haberman, Maggie, and Alan Feuer. "Invited Over to Trump's, an Outcast Rapper Brings Along a White Supremacist." *New York Times*, November 26, 2022, A20.

Haberman, Maggie, and Jonathan Swan. "Trump Had Wanted Activist Who Targets Muslims." *New York Times*, April 8, 2023, A15.

Hackworth, Jason. *Manufacturing Decline: How Racism and the Conservative Movement Crush the American Rust Belt*. New York: Columbia University Press, 2019.

Hanley, Richard. *The Metaphysics of Star Trek*. New York: Basic, 1997.

Heale, M. J. *McCarthy's Americans: Red Scare Politics in State and Nation, 1935–1965*. Athens: University of Georgia Press, 1998.

Herf, Jeffrey. *The Jewish Enemy: Nazi Propaganda during World War II and the Holocaust*. Cambridge, MA: Belknap, 2008.

Horkheimer, Max. *Critique of Instrumental Reason*, trans. Matthew O'Connell. New York: Verso, 2013 [1974].

Houlgate, Stephen. *Hegel's 'Phenomenology of Spirit': A Reader's Guide*. New York: Bloomsbury Academic, 2013.

Howe, Ben Ryder. "Scouting Out The Next Wave Of Robot Workers." *New York Times*, July 30, 2023, BU6.

Hurdle, Jon. "Philadelphia Forges Plan to Rebuild From Decay." *New York Times*, January 1, 2014, B1.

Hurtado, Albert L. *Intimate Frontiers: Sex, Gender, and Culture in Old California*. Albuquerque: University of New Mexico Press, 1999.

Israel, Jonathan I. *Radical Enlightenment: Philosophy and the Making of Modernity, 1650–1750.* New York: Oxford University Press, 2001.

Israel, Jonathan I. *Enlightenment Contested: Philosophy, Modernity, and the Emancipation of Man, 1670–1752.* New York: Oxford University Press, 2006.

Israel, Jonathan I. *The Expanding Blaze: How the American Revolution Ignited the World, 1775–1848.* Princeton: Princeton University Press, 2017.

Johnson, Geraldine A. *Renaissance Art: A Very Short Introduction.* New York: Oxford University Press, 2005.

Jones, Gareth Stedman. *Karl Marx: Greatness and Illusion.* Cambridge: Cambridge University Press, 2016.

Jones, Paul. *Critical Theory and Demagogic Populism.* Manchester: Manchester University Press, 2021.

Kading, Terry. "Drawn into 9/11, But Where Have all the Superheroes Gone?" In *Comics as Philosophy*, ed. Jeff McLaughlin. Jackson: University of Mississippi, 2005.

Kallis, Aristotle A. *Nazi Propaganda and the Second World War.* New York: Palgrave Macmillan, 2008.

Kant, Immanuel. *Critique of the Power of Judgment*, rev. ed. New York: Cambridge University Press, 2001[1790].

Kant, Immanuel. *Critique of Pure Reason*, trans. Max Muller. New York: Penguin, 2008 [1781].

Kara, Siddharth. *Modern Slavery: A Global Perspective.* New York: Columbia University Press, 2017.

Karni, Annie. "Far-Right Republicans Face Tough Races in Swing Districts, Testing McCarthy." *New York Times*, October 16, 2022, A29

Kaveney, Roz. *Superheroes! Capes and Crusaders in Comics and Films.* New York: I.B. Tauris, 2008.

Keller, Michael H., and David D. Kirkpatrick. "Suspicion and Blame as Their America Vanishes." *New York Times*, October 24, 2022, A1.

Klein, Matthew C., and Michael Pettis. *Trade Wars Are Class Wars: How Rising Inequality Distorts the Global Economy and Threatens International Peace.* New Haven: Yale University Press, 2020.

Klein, Michael. "Historical Memory, Film, and the Vietnam Era." In *From Hanoi to Hollywood: The Vietnam War in American Film*, ed. Linda Dittmar and Gene Michaud. New Brunswick: Rutgers University Press, 1990.

Kolker, Robert P. *Triumph over Containment: American Film in the 1950s.* New Brunswick, NJ: Rutgers University Press, 2022.

Kracauer, Siegfriend. *From Caligari to Hitler: A Psychological History of the German Film.* Princeton: Princeton University Press, 2004 [1947].

Kreines, James. *Reason in the World: Hegel's Metaphysics and Its Philosophical Appeal.* New York: Oxford University Press, 2015.

Kristof, Nicholas. "Trump Calls On Extremists To 'Stand By'." *New York Times*, October 1, 2020, A27.

Kumar, Anita. "Decoding Trump's Speech before the United Nations." *Politico*, September 24, 2019. Web.

Kuo, Christopher. "Kevin Spacey, Facing Trial in London, Plans a Return to Acting." *New York Times*, June 16, 2023, C4.

Kutulas, Judy. *After Aquarius Dawned: How the Revolutions of the Sixties Became the Popular Culture of the Seventies*. Chapel Hill: University of North Carolina Press, 2017.

Le Blanc, Paul, Alan Wald, and George Breitman, eds. *Trotskyism in the United States: Historical Essays and Reconsiderations*, 2nd ed. Chicago: Haymarket Books, 2016.

Leonhardt, David. "Trump Encourages Violence." *New York Times*, March 18, 2019, A23.

Leonhardt, David. "Democracy Challenged." *New York Times*, September 18, 2022, A1.

Lerner, Gerda. *The Creation of Patriarchy*. New York: Oxford University Press, 1986.

Levine, Lawrence. *Highbrow/Lowbrow: The Emergence of Cultural Hierarchy in America*. Cambridge, MA: Harvard University Press, 1990.

Liptak, Adam. "This Clash Might Have Made the Framers Gasp." *New York Times*, May 8, 2019, A1.

Liptak, Adam, and Nick Corasaniti. "Supreme Court Could Reshape Election Rules." *New York Times*, July 1, 2022, A1.

Lohr, Steve. "A.I. Threatens Lawyers? We've Heard This Before." *New York Times*, April 10, 2023, B1.

Madrigal, Alexis C. "The Computer That Predicted the U.S. Would Win the Vietnam War." *The Atlantic*, October 5, 2017. Web.

Marciano, John. *The American War in Vietnam: Crime or Commemoration?* New York: Monthly Review, 2016.

Martin, Lerone A. *The Gospel of J. Edgar Hoover: How the FBI Aided and Abetted the Rise of White Christian Nationalism*. Princeton: Princeton University Press, 2023.

Marx, Karl. *On the Jewish Question*. 1844, http://www.marxists.org/archive/marx/works/1844/jewish-question/.

Marx, Karl. *The Critique of the Gotha Programme*. London: Electric Book Co., 2001 [1875].

Mazzetti, Mark. "Senate Drops Bid to Report on Drone Use." *New York Times* April 29, 2014, A10.

Mazzetti, Mark. "Panel Faults C.I.A. Over Brutality Toward Terrorism Suspects." *New York Times*, December 10, 2014, A1.

McFadden, Robert D. "John M. Patterson, 99, Governor Who Backed Klan in Alabama, Dies." *New York Times*, June 7, 2021, A22.

McGilligan, Patrick, and Paul Buhle. *Tender Comrades: A Backstory of the Hollywood Blacklist*. New York: St. Martin's Press, 1997.

McKee, Guin A. *The Problem of Jobs: Liberalism, Race, and Deindustrialization in Philadelphia*. Chicago: University of Chicago Press, 2009.

McMahon, Robert J. *The Cold War: A Very Short Introduction*, 2nd ed. New York: Oxford University Press, 2021.

McPherson, James M. *Abraham Lincoln and the Second American Revolution*. New York: Oxford University Press, 1992.

Michaels, Jonathan. *McCarthyism: The Realities, Delusions and Politics Behind the 1950s Red Scare*. New York: Routledge, 2017.

Miller, Carol Poh, and Robert Wheeler. *Cleveland: A Concise History*. Bloomington: Indiana University Press, 2009.

Moland, Lydia L. *Hegel's Aesthetics: The Art of Idealism*. New York: Oxford University Press, 2019.

Moore, Matt. "Global Military Spending Soars." Associated Press, June 9, 2004. Web.

Mosley, Layna. *Global Capital and National Governments*. Cambridge: Cambridge University Press, 2003.

Nash, Susie. *Northern Renaissance Art*. New York: Oxford University Press, 2009.

Nelson, James Carl. *The Polar Bear Expedition: The Heroes of America's Forgotten Invasion of Russia, 1918–1919*. New York: William Morrow, 2019.

Neumann, Tracy. *Remaking the Rust Belt: The Postindustrial Transformation of North America*. Philadelphia: University of Pennsylvania Press, 2016.

Nichols, Nichelle. *Beyond Uhura – Star Trek and Other Memories*. New York: G. P. Putnam's Sons, 1994.

Nielsen, Kim E. *Money, Marriage, and Madness: Tshe Life of Anna Ott*. Urbana: University of Illinois Press, 2020.

Noam, Eli M., and The International Media Concentration Collaboration. *Who Owns the World's Media?: Media Concentration and Ownership around the World*. New York: Oxford University Press, 2016.

Oakes, James. *Freedom National: The Destruction of Slavery in the United States*. New York: W.W. Norton & Company, 2012.

Olsen, Mary-Elizabeth. *Nazi Cinema as Entertainment: The Politics of Entertainment in the Third Reich*. Rochester, NY: Camden House, 2004.

Ong, Walter. "The Comics and the Super State." In *The Superhero Reader*, ed. Charles Hatfield, Jeet Heer, and Kent Worcester. Jackson: University Press of Mississippi, 2013.

Oshinsky, David M. *A Conspiracy So Immense: The World of Joe McCarthy*. New York: Oxford University Press, 2005.

Ownby, Ted, ed. *Manners and Southern History*. Jackson: University Press of Mississippi, 2011.

Ozersky, Josh. *Archie Bunker's America: TV in an Era of Change, 1968–1978*. Carbondale: Southern Illinois University Press, 2003.

Page, Benjamin I., Jason Seawright, and Matthew J. Lacombe. *Billionaires and Stealth Politics*. Chicago: University of Chicago Press, 2018.

Palmer, Bryan D. *James P. Cannon and the Origins of the American Revolutionary Left, 1890–1928*. Urbana: University of Illinois Press, 2010.

Palmer, Bryan D. *James P. Cannon and the Emergence of Trotskyism in the United States, 1928–38*. Boston: Brill, 2022.

Paolucci, Henry. "Introduction" in *Hegel: On the Arts*, Henry Paolucci, ed., 2nd ed. Smyrna, DE: Griffon House, 2001.

Patel, Kiran Klaus. *The New Deal: A Global History*. Princeton: Princeton University Press, 2016.

Paybarah, Azi. "Texas G.O.P. Adopts Stolen Election Claims." *New York Times*, June 20, 2022, A13.

Perkins, Robert L., ed. *History and System: Hegel's Philosophy of History*. Albany: State University of New York, 1984.

Pickard, Victor. *Democracy without Journalism?: Confronting the Misinformation Society*. New York: Oxford University Press, 2020.

Piketty, Thomas. *Capital in the Twenty-First Century*, trans. Arthur Goldhammer. Cambridge, MA: Belknap Press, 2014.

Pippin, Robert B. *Philosophy by Other Means: The Arts in Philosophy and Philosophy in the Arts*. Chicago: University of Chicago Press, 2021.

Popkin, Jeremy D. *A New World Begins: The History of the French Revolution*. New York: Basic Books, 2019.

Prados, John. *The Family Jewels: The CIA, Secrecy, and Presidential Power*. Austin: University of Texas Press, 2013.

Prime, Rebecca. *Hollywood Exiles in Europe: The Blacklist and Cold War Film Culture*. New Brunswick, NJ: Rutgers University Press, 2014.

Qiu, Linda. "How Bragg And Soros Are Linked." *New York Times*, March 24, 2023, A16.

Rancière, Jacques. *Aesthetics and Its Discontents*, trans. Steve Corcoran. Malden, MA: Polity, 2009.

Rappeport, Alan, and Jim Tankersley. "U.S. Debt Surpasses $31 Trillion." *New York Times*, October 5, 2022, B1.

Rauchway, Eric. *The Great Depression and the New Deal: A Very Short Introduction*. New York: Oxford University Press, 2009.

Reel, Monte. *A Brotherhood of Spies: The U-2 and the CIA's Secret War*. New York: Doubleday, 2018.

Regalado, Aldo. "Modernity, Race, and the American Superhero." In *Comics as Philosophy*, ed. Jeff McLaughlin. Jackson: University of Mississippi, 2005.

Rentschler, Eric. *The Ministry of Illusion: Nazi Cinema and Its Afterlife*. Cambridge, MA: Harvard University Press, 1996.

Reynolds, Richard. *Super Heroes: A Modern Mythology*. Jackson: University Press of Mississippi, 1992.

Riggleman, Denver, and Hunter Walker. *The Breach: The Untold Story of the Investigation into January 6th*. New York: Henry Holt, 2022.

Risen, James, and Mark Mazetti. "Case Ends Against Ex-Blackwater Officials." *New York Times*, February 22, 2013, A16.

Robinson, William I. *A Theory of Global Capitalism: Production, Class, and State in a Transnational World*. Baltimore: Johns Hopkins University Press, 2004.

Rockmore, Tom. *Marx's Dream: From Capitalism to Communism*. Chicago: University of Chicago Press, 2018.

Roose, Kevin. "What Is QAnon, the Conspiracy Swarm?" *New York Times*, August 19, 2020, B1.

Rosenberg, Carol. "War Crimes Hearing Revisits Abuses Meted by U.S. Troops." *New York Times*, May 2, 2022, A8.

Rosenberg, Carol. "Psychologist Describes Fearing for Prisoner at C.I.A. Black Site." *New York Times*, May 4, 2022, A22.

Rosenberg, Carol. "Guantánamo's Oldest Prisoner, Never Charged, Is Released and Returns to Pakistan." *New York Times*, October 30, 2022, A27.

Rosenberg, Carol. "U.N. Rebukes U.S. Torture Of Saudi Man At Cuba Base." *New York Times*, June 5, 2023, A10.

Rosenberg, Carol. "Judge to Decide Whether C.I.A. Torture's Taint Stretched to Guantánamo." *New York Times*, July 1, 2023, A20.

Ryerson, James. "Harry G. Frankfurt, a Philosopher Eager to Cut the Bull, Dies at 94." *New York Times*, July 18, 2023, A17.

Salam, Maya. "Years Later, 'Seinfeld' Resonates." *New York Times*, May 15, 2023, C1.

Sanger, David E. "Rebel Arms Flow Is Said to Benefit Jihadists in Syria." *New York Times*, October 15, 2012, A1.

Sanger, David E., and Peter Baker. "Obama Limits When U.S. Would Use Nuclear Arms." *New York Times*, April 6, 2010, A1.

Savage, Charlie. "Order Limits Report of Deaths From U.S. Airstrikes." *New York Times*, March 7, 2019, A14.

Savage, Charlie, and Maggie Haberman. "An Advocate of Presidential Power Interests Trump for Attorney General." *New York Times*, December 7, 2018, A15.

Savage, William J. *Comic Books and America, 1945–1954*. Norman: University of Oklahoma Press, 1990.

Schecter, Darrow. *The Critique of Instrumental Reason from Weber to Habermas*. New York: Bloomsbury Academic, 2012.

Schmitt, Eric, Thomas Gibbons-Neff, Charlie Savage, and Helene Cooper. "Trump Is Said to Plan Reduction of Forces in Afghanistan, Iraq and Somalia." *New York Times*, November 17, 2020, A13.

Schmidt, Michael S., and Maggie Haberman. "First Amendment is Likely Linchpin of Trump Defense." *New York Times*, Aug. 3, 2023, A1.

Schulte-Sasse, Linda. *Entertaining the Third Reich: Illusions of Wholeness in Nazi Cinema*. Durham: Duke University Press, 1996.

Schulzinger, Robert D. *A Time for War: The United States and Vietnam, 1941–1975*. New York: Oxford University Press, 1999.

Seed, David. *Science Fiction: A Very Short Introduction*. New York: Oxford University Press, 2011.

Seefedt, Kristin S., and John D. Graham. *America's Poor and the Great Recession*. Bloomington: Indiana University Press, 2013.

Shambaugh, David. *China Goes Global: The Partial Power*. Oxford University Press, 2013.

Shane, Scott. "C.I.A.'s History Poses Hurdles for an Obama Nominee." *New York Times*, March 7, 2012, A1.

Shane, Scott. "Portrayal of C.I.A. Torture in Bin Laden Film Reopens a Debate." *New York Times* December 13, 2012, A1.

Shane, Scott. "U.S. Practiced Torture After 9/11, Nonpartisan Review Concludes." *New York Times*, April 16, 2013, A1.

Shanker, Thom. "Proposed Military Spending Is Highest Since WWII." *New York Times*, February 4, 2008, A10.

Shear, Michael D. "Trump Imposes New Travel Ban on 7 Countries." *New York Times*, September 25, 2017, A1.

Shear, Michael D. "Trump Amplifies 'White Power' on Twitter." *New York Times*, June 29, 2020, A15.

Simons, Suzanne. *Master of War: Blackwater USA's Erik Prince and the Business of War*. New York: Harper, 2009.
Simpson, James. *Permanent Revolution: The Reformation and the Illiberal Roots of Liberalism*. Cambridge, MA: Belknap, 2019.
Sinclair, Timothy J. *The New Masters of Capital: American Bond Rating Agencies and the Politics of Creditworthiness*. Ithaca: Cornell University Press, 2014.
Singer, Peter. *Marx: A Very Short Introduction*. New York: Oxford University Press, 2001.
SIPRI. *SIPRI Fact Sheet: Trends in World Military Expenditure, 2021*. Stockholm: SIPRI, April 2022. Web.
Sircello, Guy. *New Theory of Beauty*. Princeton: Princeton University Press, 2016.
Smith, Mitch. "10 Years After Filing for Bankruptcy, Detroit Has a Long To-Do List." *New York Times*, July 16, 2023, A12.
Sructon, Roger. *Beauty: A Very Short Introduction*. New York: Oxford University Press, 2011.
Staal, Jonas. *Propaganda Art in the 21st Century*. Cambridge, MA: MIT Press, 2019.
Steinhoff, James. *Automation and Autonomy: Labour, Capital and Machines in the Artificial Intelligence Industry*. New York: Palgrave Macmillan, 2021.
Stevenson, Richard W. "White House says Prisoner Policy Set Humane Tone." *New York Times*, June 23, 2005, A1.
Sugrue, Thomas J. *The Origins of the Urban Crisis: Race and Inequality in Postwar Detroit*. Princeton: Princeton University Press, 2005.
Summers, Harry G. "Body Count Proved to Be a False Prophet." *Los Angeles Times*, February 9, 1991, A5.
Surber, Jere Paul. *Culture and Critique*. New York: Routledge, 1998.
Swan, Jonathan, Charlie Savage, and Maggie Haberman. "Trump and Allies Seeking Vast Increase of His Power." *New York Times*, July 17, 2023, A1.
Swanson, Ana. "U.S. Trade Deficit Surged In 2022, Nearing $1 Trillion." *New York Times*, February 8, 2023, B3.
"Ten States Still Have Fewer Jobs Since Recession." *Reuters*, March 25, 2016.
The National Security Strategy of the United States of America. Washington, DC: The White House, September 2002.
Thompson, Stuart A. "Right-Wing Radio Sows Doubt About a Vote Yet to Take Place." *New York Times*, July 5, 2022, A1.
Thrush, Glenn. "Divisions Imperil Democracy, Garland Warns New Citizens." *New York Times*, September 18, 2022, A29.
Thrush, Glenn. "Garland Gingerly Steps Outside Comfort Zone With Trump Inquiries." *New York Times*, November 29, 2022, A15
Tonelson, Alan. *The Race To The Bottom*. New York: Basic Books, 2002.
"Trade Deficit Narrow, Countering Report of a Contraction." *New York Times*, February 9, 2013, B6.
Ullrich, Volker. *Hitler: Ascent, 1889–1939*. New York: Knof, 2016.
Valentino-DeVries, Jennifer, and Steve Eder. "Trump Backers Use 'Devil Terms' to Rally Voters." *New York Times*, October 23, 2022, A1.

Vegso, Roland. *The Naked Communist: Cold War Modernism and the Politics of Popular Culture*. New York: Fordham University Press, 2013.

Verene, Donald Phillip. *Hegel's Absolute: An Introduction to Reading the Phenomenology of Spirit*. Albany: State University New York Press, 2007.

Voss, Kimberly Wilmot. *Women Politicking Politely: Advancing Feminism in the 1960s and 1970s*. Lanham, MD: Lexington Books, 2017.

Wade, John. *The Golden Age of Science Fiction: A Journey into Space with 1950s Radio, TV, Films, Comics and Books*. Barnsley, UK: Pen and Sword History, 2019.

Walker, William T. *McCarthyism and the Red Scare: A Reference Guide*. Santa Barbara, CA: ABC-CLIO, 2011.

Wayne, Mike. "The Dialectical Image: Kant, Marx and Adorno." In *Marx at the Movies: Revisiting History, Theory and Practice*, ed. E. Mazierska and Lars Kristensen. New York: Palgrave Macmillan, 2014.

Weinberg, Carl R. *Red Dynamite: Creationism, Culture Wars, and Anticommunism in America*. Ithaca, NY: Cornell University Press, 2021.

Weisman, Jonathan. "Boebert's Call to Ilhan Over 'Suicide Bomber' Remark Shows Chasm Between Parties." *New York Times*, November 30, 2021, A20.

Weisman, Jonathan. "Fears Over Fate of Democracy Leave Voters Feeling Defeated." *New York Times*, October 23, 2022, A1.

Weisman, Jonathan. "Jewish Allies of Trump Recoil after He Hosts 2 Antisemites." *New York Times*, November 29, 2022, A1.

Weisman, Jonathan, and Andrew Higgins. "Behind Indictment, Right Wing Sees a Familiar Villain in Soros." *New York Times*, April 5, 2023, A17.

Weisman, Jonathan, and Catie Edmondson. "Republican Censured By a Divided House For a Violent Video." *New York Times*, November 18, 2021, A14.

Welch, David. *Propaganda and the German Cinema, 1933–1945*. New York: Oxford University Press, 2001.

Welch, David. *The Third Reich: Politics and Propaganda*, 2nd ed. New York: Routledge, 2002.

Welch, Evelyn. *Art in Renaissance Italy: 1350–1500*. New York: Oxford University Press, 2001.

Whitfield, Stephen E., with Gene Roddenberry. *The Making of Star Trek*. New York: Ballantine Books, 1968.

Wiedenfeld, Grant. *Hollywood Sports Movies and the American Dream*. New York: Oxford University Press, 2022.

Willbanks, James. *The Tet Offensive: A Concise History*. New York: Colombia University Press, 2008.

Williams, T. C. *The Concept of the Categorical Imperative: A Study of the Place of the Categorical Imperative in Kant's Ethical Theory*. New York: Clarendon Press, 1968.

Williams, Timothy. "For Shrinking Cities, Destruction Is a Path to Renewal." *New York Times*, November 12, 2013, A15.

Wines, Michael, and Adam Liptak. "Justice Dept. Reaffirms Goal For the Census." *New York Times*, July 6, 2019, A1.

Wingfield, Nick, and Patricia Cohen. "Let the Bidding Begin." *New York Times*, September 8, 2017, B1.

Woods, Jeff. *Black Struggle, Red Scare: Segregation and Anti-Communism in the South, 1948–1968*. Baton Rouge: Louisiana State University, 2004.

Yager, Edward M. *Ronald Reagan's Journey: Democrat to Republican*. Lanham, MD: Rowman & Littlefield, 2006.

Yalom, Marilyn. *A History of the Wife*. New York: HarperCollins, 2001

Zelizer, Julian E., ed. In *The Presidency of Donald J. Trump: A First Historical Assessment*. Princeton: Princeton University Press, 2022.

INDEX

A

"A Better World" (2003) (*Justice League*), 75
"Alive!" (2006) (*Justice League Unlimited*), 76
Apocalypse Now (1979), 28, 29, 30, 31
"Archie and the KKK" (1977) (*All in the Family*), 11
Archie Bunker's Place (1979–1983), 10-11

B

"Bar Association" (1996) (*Star Trek: Deep Space Nine*), 65n13
"Bem" (1974) (*Star Trek: The Animated Series*), 12
Biden, Joe (U.S. presidential administration), 85–86
Bloomberg, Michael, 73
Born on the Fourth of July (1989), 29

"Bread and Circuses" (1968) (*Star Trek*), 54
Bush, George W. (U.S. presidential administration), 41, 73–74, 81

C

"City on the Edge of Forever" (1967) (*Star Trek*), 17, 43, 52, 63-64
"Court Martial" (1967) (*Star Trek*), 42–43, 45, 47, 52, 56

D

Das Herz der Königin (1940), 26
"Day of the Dove" (1968) (*Star Trek*), 29, 39–40, 41, 47, 50, 52, 58
Der Fuchs von Glenarvon (1940), 26
Destination Moon (1950), 38, 39n11
Die Rothchilds Aktien auf Waterloo (1940), 24–25

E

"Elaan of Troyius" (1968) (*Star Trek*), 50, 52, 53–54
"Errand of Mercy" (1967) (*Star Trek*), 32n34

F

Father Knows Best (1954–1960), 49-50
"Flashpoint" (2005) (*Justice League Unlimited*), 72, 80
"Friday's Child" (1967) (*Star Trek*), 54
Full Metal Jacket (1987), 29, 30

G

"Galileo Seven" (1967) (*Star Trek*), 28, 29–30, 32–33
"George and the President" (1976) (*The Jeffersons*), 11

H

Hamburger Hill (1987), 29,30, 33–34
Hegel, Georg, 2
Heimkehr (1941), 26
"Homefront" (1996) (*Star Trek: Deep Space Nine*), 70
Hoover, J. Edgar, 39, 40
House of Cards (2013–2018), 8
"How Sharper Than a Serpent's Tooth" (1974) (*Star Trek: The Animated Series*), 13

I

"In the Cards" (1997) (*Star Trek: Deep Space Nine*), 62
Invaders from Mars (1953), 39
Invasion of the Body Snatchers (1956), 39, 42
"Is There in Truth No Beauty?" (1968) (*Star Trek*), 53
It Came from Outer Space (1953), 39

J

Jud Süs (1940), 23–24
Julia (1968–1971), 50
"Justice" (1987) (*Star Trek: The Next Generation*), 2–3
Justice League: The New Frontier (2008), 44

L

"Let that Be your Last Battlefield" (1969) (*Star Trek*), 50, 56–58
"Little Green Men" (1995) (*Star Trek: Deep Space Nine*), 62
"Look Me In the Eye" (2021) (*Hanna*), 16n32
"Looking for Loans in All the Wrong Places" (*Roseanne*), 10

M

Marx, Karl, 13, 62
Mary Tyler Moore (1970–1977), 50–51, 55
Mein Leben für Irland (1941), 26
"Metamorphosis" (2002) (*Justice League*), 78
"Mirror, Mirror" (1967) (*Star Trek*), 45
"Mudd's Women" (1966) (*Star Trek*), 54

N

"Nothing Like It in the World" (2020) (*The Boys*), 70, 72, 75

O

Obama, Barak (U.S. presidential administration), 74
Ohm Krüger (1941), 26

P

"Paradise Lost" (1996) (*Star Trek: Deep Space Nine*), 70
"Past Tense" (1995) (*Star Trek: Deep Space Nine*), 9, 63–65
"Patriot Act" (2006), (*Justice League Unlimited*), 81–82
"Patterns of Force" (1968) (*Star Trek*), 40
Patton (1970), 29
Platoon (1986), 28, 29, 30, 31
"Private Little War" (1968) (*Star Trek*), 28, 31–32, 43–44

Q

"Question Authority" (2005) (*Justice League Unlimited*), 75, 80, 82

R

Reagan, Ronald, 42
Rivera, Diego, 13–14
Roddenberry, Gene, 38
"Room For Growth" (2022) (*Star Trek: Lower Decks*), 62

S

"Sacred Ground" (1996) (*Star Trek: Voyager*), 3
"School of Hard Knocks" (2018) (*Blue Bloods*), 77
Seinfeld (1989–1998), 8
Slap Shot (1977), 9
Snyder, Daniel, 73
"Stretch Cunningham, Goodbye" (1977) (*All in the Family*), 11
Superman: Red Son (2020), 20–21

T

The Adventures of Huckberry Finn, 10
"The Appendectomy" (1979) (*All in the Family*), 11
"The Big Ride" (2020) (*The Boys*), 72
"The Bloody Doors Off" (2020) (*The Boys*), 71
"The Cage" (pilot) (*Star Trek*), 8
"The Cloud Minders" (1969) (*Star Trek*), 14–15, 50, 58
"The Dark Ages" (1992) (*Roseanne*), 9
The Day the Earth Stood Still (1951), 43–44, 47
"The Doomsday Sanction" (2005) (*Justice League Unlimited*), 74, 80, 81, 82
"The Enterprise Incident" (1968) (*Star Trek*), 51
"The Eye of the Beholder" (1974), (*Star Trek: The Animated Series*), 12
The Green Berets (1968), 28, 34, 35
"The Magicks of Megas-Tu" (1973) (*Star Trek: The Animated Series*), 12
"The Man Trap" (1966) (*Star Trek*), 53
The Matrix (1999), 7
"The Menagerie" (1966) (*Star Trek*), 8
"The Name of the Game" (2019) (*The Boys*), 73
"The Neutral Zone" (1988) (*Star Trek: The Next Generation*), 61–62
"The Omega Glory" (1968) (*Star Trek*), 42, 47, 64
The Red Planet Mars (1952), 45, 47
"The Return of the Archons" (1967) (*Star Trek*), 41–42
"The Savage Curtain" (1969) (*Star Trek*), 46–47, 50, 64

"The Ties That Bind" (2005) (*Justice League Unlimited*), 75
"The Ultimate Computer" (1968) (*Star Trek*), 56
Theory of the Unitary Executive, 73–74
"There Is a Tide…" (2021) (*Star Trek: Discovery*), 62
Three's Company (1977–1984), 11
"Time Amok" (1967) (*Star Trek*), 51–52
"To Another Shore" (2005) (*Justice League Unlimited*), 72, 74
Tour of Duty (1987–1990), 31
"Transfigurations" (1990) (*Star Trek: The Next Generation*), 15–16
Trotsky, Leon, 61, 64
"True Believer" (2021) (*The Equalizer*), 10
Trump, Donald J. (former U.S. President), 16, 70, 71, 74, 75, 77, 85, 86
"Turnabout Intruder" (1969) (*Star Trek*), 50, 51, 54–55

"Twilight" (2003) (*Justice League*), 76

W

"Walk Out" (1989) (*Wonder Years*), 34
"War World" (2002) (*Justice League*), 76–77
"We Gotta Go Now" (2020) (*The Boys*), 70, 74
"What I Know" (2020) (*The Boys*), 73
"Whom Gods Destroy" (1969) (*Star Trek*), 45
"Wink of an Eye" (1968) (*Star Trek*), 52

Z

Zero Dark Thirty (2012), 80–81

PETER LANG
PROMPT

Peter Lang Prompts offer our authors the opportunity to publish original research in small volumes that are shorter and more affordable than traditional academic monographs. With a faster production time, this concise model gives scholars the chance to publish time-sensitive research, open a forum for debate, and make an impact more quickly. Like all Peter Lang publications, Prompts are thoroughly peer reviewed and can even be included in series.

For further information, please contact:

editorial@peterlang.com

To order, please contact our Customer Service Department:

peterlang@presswarehouse.com (within the U.S.)
orders@peterlang.com (outside the U.S.)

Visit our website: www.peterlang.com

Prompts include:

Claudia Aburto Guzmán, *Poesía reciente de voces en diálogo con la ascendencia hispano-hablante en los Estados Unidos: Antología breve*. ISBN 978-1-4331-5207-8. 2020

William Robert Adamson, *Mine Own Familiar Friend: The Relationship between Gerard Hopkins and Robert Bridges*. ISBN 978-1-80079-485-6. 2021

Tywan Ajani, *Barriers to Rebuilding the African American Community: Understanding the Issues Facing Today's African Americans from a Social Work Perspective*. ISBN 978-1-4331-7681-4. 2020

Macarena Areco, *Bolaño Constelaciones: Literatura, sujetos, territories*. ISBN 978-1-4331-7575-6. 2020

Robin Burgess (ed.), *FRANCESCO ALGAROTTI: AN ESSAY ON THE OPERA (Saggio sopra l'opera in musica) The editions of 1755 and 1763*. ISBN 978-1-80079-505-1. 2022

Desrine Bogle. *The Transatlantic Culture Trade: Caribbean Creole Proverbs from Africa, Europe, and the Caribbean*. ISBN 978-1-4331-5723-3. 2020

Jean-François Caron. *Irresponsible Citizenship: The Cultural Roots of the Crisis of Authority in Times of Pandemic*. ISBN 978-1-4331-8908-1. 2021

Jean-François Caron, *The Great Lockdown: Western Societies and the Fear of Death*. ISBN 978-1-4331-9535-8. 2022

Marcílio de Freitas and Marilene Corrêa da Silva Freitas, *The Future of Amazonia in Brazil: A Worldwide Tragedy*. ISBN 978-1-4331-7793-4. 2020

Mihai Dragnea. *Christian Identity Formation Across the Elbe in the Tenth and Eleventh Centuries.* Christianity and Conversion in Scandinavia and the Baltic Region, c. 800–1600, vol. 1. ISBN 978-1-4331-8431-4. 2021

Janet Farrell Leontiou, *The Doctor Still Knows Best: How Medical Culture Is Still Marked by Paternalism.* Health Communication, vol. 15. ISBN 978-1-4331-7322-6. 2020

Clare Gorman (ed.), *Miss-representation: Women, Literature, Sex and Culture.* ISBN 978-1-78874-586-4. 2020

Eva Marín Hlynsdóttir. *Gender in Organizations: The Icelandic Female Council Manager.* ISBN 978-1-4331-7729-3. 2020

Micol Kates, *Towards a Vegan-Based Ethic: Dismantling Neo-Colonial Hierarchy Through an Ethic of Lovingkindness.* ISBN 978-1-4331-7797-2. 2020

Sunho Kim, *Inner Mongolia, Outer Mongolia: The History of the Division of the "Descendants of Chinggis Khan" in the 20th Century.* ISBN 978-1-4331-8185-6. 2022

Feridoon Koohi-Kamali (ed.), *Exploring Roots of Inequality in Latin America and Peru.* ISBN 978-1-4331-8989-0. 2021

Guy Merchant, Cathy Burnett, Jeannie Bulman, and Emma Rogers. *Stacking Stories: Exploring the Hinterland of Education.* ISBN 978-1-80079-686-7. 2022

Matt Qvortrup, *Winners and Losers: Which Countries are Successful and Why?.* ISBN 978-1-80079-405-4. 2021

Peter Raina, *Doris Lessing – A Life Behind the Scenes: The Files of the British Intelligence Service MI5.* ISBN 978-1-80079-183-1. 2021

Peter Raina (trans.), *Heinrich von Kleist Poems.* ISBN 978-1-80079-043-8. 2020

Josiane Ranguin, *Mediating the Windrush Children: Caryl Phillips and Horace Ové.* ISBN 978-1-4331-7424-7. 2020

Dylan Scudder, *Coffee and Conflict in Colombia: Part of the Pentalemma Series on Managing Global Dilemmas.* ISBN 978-1-4331-7568-8. 2020

Dylan Scudder, *Conflict Minerals in the Democratic Republic of Congo: Part of the Pentalemma Series on Managing Global Dilemmas.* ISBN 978-1-4331-7561-9. 2020

Dylan Scudder, *Mining Conflict in the Philippines: Part of the Pentalemma Series on Managing Global Dilemmas.* ISBN 978-1-4331-7632-6. 2020

Dylan Scudder, *Multi-Hazard Disaster in Japan: Part of the Pentalemma Series on Managing Global Dilemmas.* ISBN 978-1-4331-7530-5. 2020

Wesley A. Stroud, *Education for Liberation, Education for Dignity: The Story of St. Monica's School of Basic Learning for Women.* ISBN 978-1-4331-7911-2. 2021

Geanneti Tavares Salomon, *Fashion and Irony in «Dom Casmurro».* ISBN 978-1-78997-972-5. 2021

Zia Ul Haque Shamsi, *South Asia Needs Hybrid Peace.* ISBN 978-1-4331-9422-1. 2022

Mohammad Rafiqul Islam Talukdar, *Local Government Budgetary Autonomy: Evidence from Bangladesh.* ISBN 978-1-80079-528-0. 2022

Shai Tubali, *Cosmos and Camus: Science Fiction Film and the Absurd.* ISBN 978-1-78997-664-9. 2020

Angela Williams, *Hip Hop Harem: Women, Rap and Representation in the Middle East.* ISBN 978-1-4331-7295-3. 2020

Ivan Zhavoronkov (trans.), *The Socio-Cultural and Philosophical Origins of Science* by Anatoly Nazirov. ISBN 978-1-4331-7228-1. 2020